Canadian Student Information (CSI) Document

to accompany

Understanding Nutrition
11th Edition

THOMSON

—★—™

NELSON

ISBN-13: 978-0-17-646426-4
ISBN-10: 0-17-646426-3

This textbook is a Nelson custom publication. Because your instructor has chosen to produce a custom publication, you pay only for material that you will use in your course.

Acknowledgements:

Many thanks to Alicia C Garcia PhD RD CFE for coauthoring the companion CSI document that accompanies the 10th edition of Nutrition: *Concepts and Controversies*, some of which were used for this CSI document.

I would like to thank my son, Leonard Alan Piché Jr HBSc, BEd for compiling the majority of the weblinks for the Back-of-the-Book CD for this CSI doc, excellent work Len!

Contents

....

....

Introduction

This supplement is designed to provide you with Canadian Nutrition information that is current and accurate, when this information differs from that from the United States. This includes issues such as food labelling, nutrition and physical activity guidelines and recommendations, nutrition and health programs, nutrition and physical activity education tools and resources including clinical practice guidelines. Currently, many policies and standards of Canada and the United States are becoming harmonized, such as the Dietary Reference Intakes. Canadian nutrition educators and colleagues in the United States use a common research base for describing how nutrients function in the body and for planning nutrition interventions. However, differences in food intake patterns, health statistics, and health policy affect the content and format of nutrition programs.

While you may have Internet access to much of the Canadian information, along with similar information for the United States and many other countries of the world, you may often have difficulty sorting out the Canadian materials from those of other countries because of global access to information through the media. This supplement identifies Canadian regulations, standards, programs, research and resources according to the topics discussed in each chapter or highlighted in *Understanding Nutrition, Eleventh Edition*. It is my hope that using the information in this supplement will make your study of Nutrition more relevant, interesting and applicable to your lives here in Canada.

Chapter 1 Canadian Information (An Overview of Nutrition)

1-1   Dietary Guidelines

Canada's equivalent to the Dietary Guidelines for Americans (see **Table 2.1** of the textbook) were Canada's Guidelines for Healthy Eating (see **Table 2.2** of the textbook), which was developed by the Health and Welfare Communications/ Implementation Committee[1]. The guidelines were the messages designed to help consumers achieve the Scientific Review Committee's Nutrition Recommendations for Canadians, which were developed for health professionals and the food industry[2]. The Nutrition Recommendations for Canadians are similar to those for the U.S. since both countries now base most recommendations on the Institute of Medicine's Dietary Reference Intakes (1997-2005) reports. The Office of Nutrition Policy and Promotion, Health Canada is leading the review of Canada's Dietary Guidance system, including the Nutrition Recommendations for Canadians. Health Canada recently indicated that as a result of a number of factors, including stakeholder feedback, these latter recommendations will not be updated, , however, key healthy eating messages have been included the 'new' Canada's Food Guide released in February 2007. In addition, some of the 'older' nutrition recommendations e.g., on fat intake are being replaced with 'newer' recommendations, such as, an Acceptable Macronutrient Distribution Range of 20 – 35 per cent of total calories from fat for adults. This and other 'newer' recommendations are based on the recent Dietary Reference Intake (DRI) reports developed by committees of American and Canadian nutritional scientists with guidance by the U.S. Food and Nutrition Board of the Institute of Medicine and have now been adopted by Health Canada.

You can check the Health Canada web site for current information about the review process
http://www.hc-sc.gc.ca/fn-an/nutrition/diet-guide-nutri/nut_pol_diet_guid-pol_nut_lig_direc_e.html

Dietary Guidelines for many countries, including ours, contain a statement about the importance of physical activity. Use Canada's targeted Physical Activity Guides (see http://www.phac-aspc.gc.ca/pau-uap/fitness/index.html) to help you enjoy physical activity everyday. Further more, the 2002/2003 CCHS not only revealed the good news that physical inactivity decreased between the late 1990s and 2002 it also revealed that much work remained because an estimated 51% of Canadian adults were still physically inactive (http://www.cflri.ca/eng/statistics/surveys/pam2004.php). The report further indicated that more women than men are physically inactive and that physical inactivity increases with age. These latter results prompted an almost immediate response from the Ministers responsible for Physical Activity, Recreation and Sport in 2003 who set a goal to reduce physical inactivity by 10% by 2010 (http://www.phac-aspc.gc.ca/hl-vs-strat/). More recently, in the fall of 2005, they also approved "The Integrated Pan-Canadian Healthy Living Strategy" which includes a new set of targets for increases in healthy eating, physical activity and healthy weights by 2015 (see below).

"The Integrated Pan-Canadian Healthy Living Strategy" 2005 targets are:

Healthy Eating
By 2015, increase by 20% the proportion of Canadians who make healthy food choices according to the Canadian Community Health Survey (CCHS), and Statistics Canada (SC)/Canadian Institute for Health Information (CIHI) health Indicators.

Physical Activity

By 2015, increase by 20% the proportion of Canadians who participate in regular physical activity based on 30 minutes/day of moderate to vigorous activity as measured by the CCHS and the Physical Activity Benchmarks/ Monitoring Program.

Healthy Weights

By 2015, increase by 20% the proportion of Canadians at a "normal" body weight based on a Body Mass Index (BMI) of 18.5 to 24.9 as measured by the National Population Health Survey (NPHS), CCHS, and SC/CIHI health indicators.

http://www.phac-aspc.gc.ca/hl-vs-strat/pdf/hls_e.pdf

1-2 Canadian Nutrition and Health Related Research

Where possible, Canadian scientists rely on Canadian data. There are a number of research papers by Canadian scientists that are useful in helping to establish new nutrition and health recommendations for Canadians. Many of these articles are published in Canadian journals, such as, the Canadian Journal of Dietetic Practice and Research, Canadian Journal of Public Health and the Journal of the Canadian Medical Association. **Table 1.3** in the textbook outlines examples of research designs being used by researchers in nutrition and health related fields and provides some strengths and weaknesses of such designs.

1-3 Leading Causes of Death in Canada

The leading causes of death in Canada tend to vary a little from those in the United States. The leading causes of death in Canada in 2001 are illustrated in the Table 1-1 below. Note that together heart disease and stroke accounted for 34 % of deaths[3]. **Table 1.5, Figure 18.2 and 18.3** of the textbook provide examples of diseases that are influenced more so by diet or genetics. Canadian students should look for the most recent statistics for nutrition-related causes of mortality through the Statistics Canada web site (www.statscan.ca).

Table 1-1 Leading Causes of Death in Canada (2001)*

Heart Disease and Stroke	74,824 (34%)
Cancer	63,774 (29%)
Respiratory Disease	22,026 (10%)
Accidents, Suicides, Violence	13,996 (6%)
All other causes	41,797 (19%)

* Modified from Statistics Canada: Major Causes of Death – Diseases of the circulatory system http://www43.statcan.ca/02/02b/02b_003_e.htm   (accessed June 25, 2007)

References Cited

[1] Health and Welfare Canada. *Action Towards Healthy Eating...Canada's Guidelines for Healthy Eating and Strategies for Implementation.* The Report of the Communications/ Implementation Committee. Ottawa: Minister of Supply and Services Canada, 1990.

[2] Health and Welfare Canada. *Nutrition Recommendations.* Ottawa: Minister of Supply and Services Canada, 1990.

[3]. from Statistics Canada: Major Causes of Death – Diseases of the circulatory system http://www43.statcan.ca/02/02b/02b_003_e.htm   (accessed June 25, 2007)

Highlight 1: Nutrition Information and Misinformation – On the Net and in the News

Sorting the Impostors from the Real Nutrition Experts

H1-1 Canadian Credible Sources of Nutrition Information

Note: According to a recent national telephone Omnibus survey conducted for the Dietitians of Canada in April 2005[1], "… 92 % of responding Canadians rated dietitians as the source of nutrition advice they trust the most" see 'Canadians trust the nutrition advice of dietitians' 06/03/05 at http://www.dietitians.ca/news/media.asp

Other Canadian credible sources of nutrition information that are similar to those listed in the **"How To"**
text box on page 33 of the textbook include - Professional health organizations, government health agencies, volunteer health agencies, and consumer groups provide consumers with reliable health and nutrition:

- **Professional health organizations, especially the Dietitians of Canada**
  http://www.dietitians.ca/ , and the Nutrition Resource Centre
  http://www.nutritionrc.ca/about.html , Canadian Medical Association (CMA)
  http://www.pslgroup.com/dg/735a.htm

- **Government health agencies such as Health Canada (HC)**
  http://www.hc-sc.gc.ca/ , Public Health Agency of Canada (PHAC)
  http://www.phac-aspc.gc.ca/new_e.html , the Canadian Health Network
  CHN http://www.canadian-health-network.ca/ , the Canadian Food
  Inspection Agency (CFIA) http://www.inspection.gc.ca/english/toce.shtml the Natural
  Health Products Directorate NHPD
  http://www.hc-sc.gc.ca/dhp-mps/prodnatur/index_e.html , Office of
  Nutrition Policy and Promotion
  http://www.hc-sc.gc.ca/ahc-asc/branch-dirgen/hpfb-dgpsa/onpp-bppn/index_e.html
  and Agriculture and Agri-Food Canada AAFC http://www.agr.gc.ca/
  Canadian Nutrient File 2005 http://www.hc-sc.gc.ca/fn-an/nutrition/fiche-nutri-data/index_e.html

- **Volunteer health agencies such as** the Heart and Stroke Foundation of
  Canada http://ww2.heartandstroke.ca/Page.asp?PageID=24 , Canadian
  Diabetes Association http://www.diabetes.ca/ , and the Canadian Cancer
  Society
  http://www.cancer.ca/ccs/internet/niw_splash/0%2C%2C3172%2C00.html

- **Reputable Industry and consumer groups such as** the Canadian Council of Food and
  Nutrition CCFN
  http://www.cancer.ca/ccs/internet/niw_splash/0%2C%2C3172%2C00.html ,
  the National Council Against Health Fraud NCAHF http://www.ncahf.org/
  and Quackwatch http://www.quackwatch.org/ .
  Consumers Association of Canada - www.consumer.ca
  Food and Consumer Products of Canada - http://www.fcpmc.com/home.asp

References

[1]. Canadians Trust the nutrition advice of Dietitans. Dietitians of Canada June 03, 2005.
http://www.dietitians.ca/news/media.asp (accessed July 06, 2006)

H1-2 Dietitians' Credentials in Canada

The qualifications for admission to Dietitians of Canada (DC) and provincial regulatory bodies are similar to those for the American Dietetic Association. DC accredits university undergraduate programs and dietetic internship programs which qualify dietitians to practise. There is no single designation of title or initials for Canadian dietitians. Provincial government legislation determines the professional designation for health professionals who practise in the province.

Alberta	- R.D. (Registered Dietitian)
British Columbia	- R.D.N. (Registered Dietitian Nutritionist)
Manitoba	- R.D. (Registered Dietitian)
New Brunswick	- P.Dt. (Professional Dietitian)
Newfoundland	- R.Dt. (Registered Dietitian)
Nova Scotia	- P.Dt. (Professional Dietitian)
Ontario	- RD (Registered Dietitian)/Dt.P. (diététiste professionnelle)
Prince Edward Island	- P.Dt. (Professional Dietitian)
Québec	- dt.p. (diététiste professionnelle)
Saskatchewan	- P.Dt. (Professional Dietitian)

To find a Registered Dietitian in your area go to
http://www.dietitians.ca/public/content/find_a_nutrition_professional/find_a_dietitian.asp

Provincial Regulatory Bodies

Provincial regulatory bodies (i.e. colleges or registration boards):
- monitor the competence of members, e.g. mandatory continuing education;
- protect the public from unsafe or unethical dietetic practice;
- protect the use of regulated title designation and initials, e.g. RD; and
- review the professional conduct of members based on complaints, and discipline members where appropriate.

The following lists the provincial regulatory bodies and their contact information in 2004. For the most current contact information, check the Dietitians of Canada web site,
http://www.dietitians.ca/public/content/career_in_nutrition/provincial_regulatory_bodies.asp.

College of Dietitians of Alberta, #540, 10707 - 100 Avenue, Edmonton, AB, T5J 3M1
Phone: 780 448-0059; Fax: 780 489-7759
Email: cda@collegeofdietitians.ab.ca
Web Site: http://collegeofdietitians.ab.ca/

British Columbia Dietitians and Nutritionists Association
401 - 1755 West Broadway, Vancouver, BC Canada V6J 4S5
Phone: 604-736-2016; Fax: 604-736-2018
Web Site: www.collegeofdietitiansbc.org

Manitoba Association of Registered Dietitians
36 - 1313 Border Street, Winnipeg, MB R3H 0X4
Phone: 204 694-0532; Fax: 204 889-1755
E-mail: mard@mts.net

New Brunswick Association of Dietitians
PO Box 22024, Landsdowne Postal Outlet, Saint John, NB E2K 4T7
Phone: 506-642-9058 (voice mail); Fax: 506-636-8900
Web Site: www.adnb-nbad.com/

Newfoundland Dietetic Association
PO Box 1756, Postal Station C, St. John's, NL A1C 5P5
Phone: 709-753-4040 or toll free at 1-877-753-4040

Nova Scotia Dietetic Association
PO Box 36104, Halifax, NS B3J 3S9
Phone: 902 454-2348; Fax: 902 461-4997 fax
E-mail: hselig@nsdassoc.ca
Web Site: www.nsdassoc.ca/

College of Dietitians of Ontario
438 University Avenue, Suite 1810, Box 40, Toronto, ON M5G 2K8
Phone: 416 598-1725; Fax: 416 598-0274
E-mail: gignacm@cdo.on.ca
Web Site: www.cdo.on.ca

Ordre professionnel des diététistes du Québec
1425 Boulevard René Levesque, oust, Bureau 703, Montréal, QC H3G 1T7
Phone: 514 393-3733; Fax: 514 393-3582
E-mail: opdq@opdq.org ;
Web Site: www.opdq.org

Saskatchewan Dietitians Association
Box 3894
Regina, SK
S4P 2R8
Phone & Fax: 306 359-3040
E-mail: registrar@saskdietitians.org
Web Site: www.saskdietitians.org

PEI Dietitians Registration Board
45 Loridale Drive, Charlottetown, PE C1E 1P2
Phone: 902 569-5184; Fax: 902 963-2933
 E-mail: schaefer@pei.sympatico.ca

Chapter 2 Canadian Information (Planning a Healthy Diet)

2-1 Daily Values on Canadian Food Labels

Daily Values are part of the Canadian nutrition labelling regulations that take effect January 1, 2006[1] for large food companies and January 1, 2008 for smaller food companies (revenues of < $1 M/yr from food sales). Thus, most pre-packaged foods will now display the mandatory Nutrition Facts table and other required nutrition information. Percentage of Daily Value (%DV) is used to express the food's content of macro-nutrients, fiber and selected vitamins and minerals, rather than using weight (g or mg). The DV reference standards for Canada are seen in Table 2-1 below. Some of the values for vitamins and minerals refer to the older Recommended Daily Intakes (RDI) values. However, the Daily Values for fat, saturated and *trans* fatty acids, carbohydrate, fiber, sodium and potassium are based on the appropriate Institute of Medicine (IOM) DRI report for a 2000 kcal diet. These differ from those listed in the textbook for the United States in that the Reference DV upon which %DV is currently calculated is different for some nutrients, the DV considers the sum of both saturated and *trans* fat, calculating a %DV for cholesterol and protein is optional.

The nutrition education program for the nutrition labelling regulations identifies that the purpose of having %DV is to show whether the food has a 'lot' or a 'little' of a nutrient in a stated amount of food. The education program is available via Health Canada, Health Products and Food Branch at http://www.hc-sc.gc.ca/hpfb-dgpsa/onpp-bppn/labelling-etiquetage/education_e.html.

Table 2-1 Canadian Reference Standard for Daily Values (based on a 2000 kCal diet) for Core Nutrients for Persons 2 Years or Older[a]

Nutrient	Amount
Fat	65 g
The sum of saturated fatty acids and *trans* fatty acids	20 g
Carbohydrate	300 g
Fibre	25 g
Cholesterol	300 mg
Sodium	2400 mg
Potassium	3500 mg
Vitamin A	1000 RE
Vitamin C	60 mg
Calcium	1100 mg
Iron	14 mg

[a] Regulations Amending the Food and Drug Regulations (Nutrition Labelling, Nutrient Content Claims and Health Claims). *Canadian Gazette Part II, Vol. 137, No. 1* pp.154-403.
http://canadagazette.gc.ca/partII/2003/20030101/pdf/g2-13701.pdf

2-2 Eating Well with Canada's Food Guide

Eating Well with Canada's Food Guide (**Appendix I, Figure I-1 of the textbook**) differs from the US Department of Agriculture's (USDA) 'new' Pyramid, MyPyramid (Figures 2.1 & 2.3 of the text book), in the number of food groups, some serving sizes and the graphic presentation. However, many of the drawbacks to MyPyramid also apply to Eating Well with Canada's Canada's Food Guide.

It is important to note: The 'new' Eating Well with Canada's Food Guide was released in February, 2007. Considerable research with consumers and nutrition educators has been completed and the results can be accessed through the web site for the Office of Nutrition Policy and Promotion, http://www.hc-sc.gc.ca/fn-an/food-guide-aliment/context/rev/rev_proc_e.html . All of the publications related to Canada's Food Guide to Healthy Eating are available from the web site. Also, a history of the food guide from '1942 to 1992' can be accessed at the following weblink http://www.hc-sc.gc.ca/fn-an/food-guide-aliment/context/hist/index_e.html .

The 'new' Canada's Food Guide is based on current nutritional science. The food intake pattern it describes meet the nutrient recommendations set out in the various recent Dietary Reference Intake reports and are consistent with the latest scientific evidence linking diet with reduced risk for the development of chronic diseases. The food guide uses a total diet approach with a broader range of servings to accommodate the nutritional needs of female and male children, teens and adults. This guide recognizes the use of foods that don't fit neatly into the four food groups and we now have an "Oils and Fats" category. **Table 2.2** below lists the Food Guide Serving recommendations for Eating Well with Canada's Food Guide for different people.

Table 2.2 Number of Food Guide Servings for Different People[b]

Food Group	Marie – 5 years old	David – 17 years old	Louise – 35 years old
Vegetables and Fruit	5	8	7-8
Grain Products	4	7	6-7
Milk and Alternatives	2	3-4	2
Meat and Alternatives	2	3	2
Oils and Fats (unsaturated)	2-3 Tbsp	2-3 Tbsp	2-3 Tbsp

[b] Eating Well with Canada's Food Guide. Minister of Health Canada, Ottawa 2007. Cat N0. H164-38/1-2007E. http://www.hc-sc.gc.ca/fn-an/food-guide-aliment/index_e.html (accessed Feb 15, 2007)

Note: Serving sizes on the Food Guide may be different from the portions listed on food labels or from those served at fast food outlets or restaurants. Also, portions are larger in North America today than in the 1970's.

Canadians can find helpful hints on 'Using the Food Guide', 'Choosing Foods', 'Maintaining Healthy Habits' etc on Health Canada's website at http://www.hc-sc.gc.ca/fn-an/food-guide-aliment/index_e.html . Your local or provincial public health department will also have copies of the 'new' Canada's Food Guide and other related resources.

Table 2-3 Eating Well with Canada's Food Guide and Support Material

- Eating Well with Canada's Food Guide
- Eating Well with Canada's Food Guide: *A Resource for Educators and Communicators* (2007)

Figure 2-1 Vegetarian Food Guide Rainbow

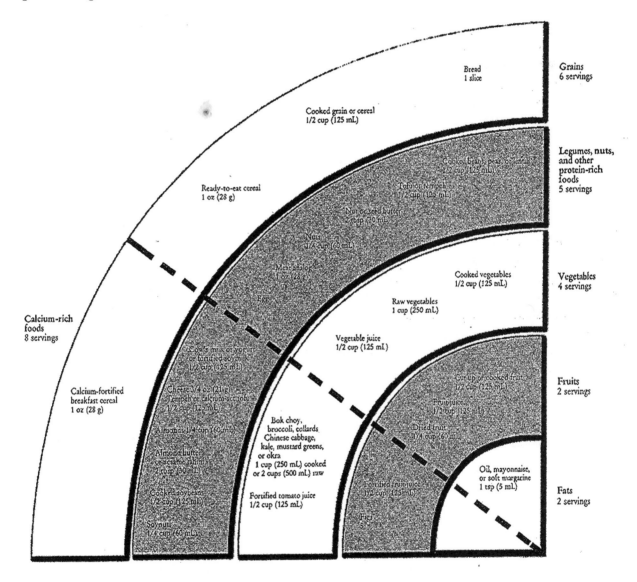

Ref. Messina, Virginia; Melina, Vesanto; Reed Mangels, Ann A New Food Guide For North American Vegetarians. Canadian Journal of Dietetic Practice and Research 2003;64:(2):pp 82-86.

Copyright 2003 Dietitians of Canada Used with permission

See also, DC Position Statement: Vegetarian Food Guide for North America

http://www.dietitians.ca/news/highlights_positions.asp?fn=view&id=2515&idstring=5019%7C3941%7C3398%7C1231%7C2482%7C2175%7C2515%7C1952%7C2516%7C2517%7C1363%7C2451%7C1188%7C1338

2-3 Canadian readings and resources

Piché, L. A. and Garcia, A. C. 2001. Factors Influencing Food-Buying Practices of Grocery Shoppers in London, Ontario. Can J Diet Prac Res 62 (4): 199-202. . A summary in lay terms also published on public access section of DC's website under News Room for Winter 2001 entitled "What Influences the Food Buying Practices of Canadian Grocery Shoppers ?"
http://www.dietitians.ca/news/highlights_research_grocery_shoppers.asp .

Garcia A C and Piché L A. 2001. Perception and Use of Canada's Food Guide to Healthy Eating by Grocery Shoppers in London, Ontario. Can J Diet Prac Res 62 (3): 123-27. A summary in lay terms also published on public access section DC's website in September 2001 under News Room entitled "What do Grocery Shoppers Think of Canada's Food Guide ?
http://www.dietitians.ca/news/highlights_research_grocery.asp

2-4 Diabetes Meal Planning Guides

The Canadian Diabetes Association recently announced their 'new' meal planning guide "Beyond the Basics: Meal Planning Guide for Healthy Eating, Diabetes Prevention and Management" to replace the "Good Health Eating Guide". It is currently available in poster format and as a 150 document (http://www.diabetes.ca/section_about/btb2006.asp) and involves a Food Group System using the exchange concept[2]. The food groups and their nutrient content are similar to those used in Quebec and the United States exchange systems and carbohydrate counting is made easier since '1 carbohydrate choice' contains about 15 g of available carbohydrate. For a list of foods that contain carbohydrates see **Appendix I (Tables I-1)** of the textbook.

Please note that there are differences compared with Canada's Food Guide when dealing with carbohydrates, lipids and proteins. This is especially important for the carbohydrate content for foods such as chocolate milk, where ½ cup (125 ml) is '1 carbohydrate choice' instead of 1 cup (250 ml) and foods are now grouped into seven food groups.

2-5 Ethnic Foods in Canada

Many of the ethnic and regional foods depicted in the Food Guides from around the world (see **Table 2.6** of the textbook for examples of Ethnic Food Choices) are eaten in Canada, as well as foods from many other countries. One of the challenges of nutrition educators working with members of the First Nations and Inuit is to recognize their traditional foods and include them with other available foods to promote healthy eating. Some education resources have been developed by nutrition educators to help address these challenges and are available through the First Nations and Inuit Health Branch (http://www.hc-sc.gc.ca/fnihb/cp/index.htm). Other adaptations of the Food Guide for different ethnic groups are also expected soon from Health Canada.

2-6 Checking Out Canadian Food Labels

Food labelling in Canada is regulated under the Food and Drugs Act and Regulations. The Canadian Food Inspection Agency enforces the food labelling regulations. The Consumer Packaging and Labelling Act and Regulations also apply to food packaging and labels. All current regulations for labelling requirements and making nutrition claims are described in 2003 The Guide to Food Labelling and Advertising[3], which can be accessed through the web site of the Canadian Food Inspection Agency, http://www.inspection.gc.ca/english/fssa/labeti/guide/toce.shtml.

With new regulations, nutrition labelling became mandatory on most food labels on January 1, 2006[1]. The new regulations also update requirements for 'nutrient content claims' (such as 'Low in Fat') and permit science-based, 'diet-related health claims' for foods. Health Canada provides an education strategy to support these regulations to help consumers make informed choices about the foods they buy and eat. Information on nutrition regulations and education program can be accessed through the Health Canada, Health Products and Food Branch at http://www.hc-sc.gc.ca/hpfb-dgpsa/onpp-bppn/labelling-etiquetage/education_e.html.

Definitions and claims under the new Canadian regulations differ in some ways from those described in the textbook for the United States. Dietitians of Canada and the Canadian Diabetes Association have developed education resources on food labelling as part of the Healthy Eating Is in Store for You program. These materials can be downloaded from: www.healthyeatingisinstore.ca.

Food Ingredients

Food ingredients are listed, using their common name, in descending order of proportion or percentage of the packaged product. For some foods, such as vegetable oils or spices, the class rather than the common name is permitted. If an ingredient is optional, or can be substituted for another one in a product, the label must list all the ingredients that are likely to be used in the product within a one-year period. The label must indicate that all of these specific ingredients may not be present in each package of the food. This is often seen on cracker labels when the source of oil or fat varies with the market availability of oil products.

At this time there is no requirement to identify food products resulting from genetic engineering (referred to in regulations as "novel foods"), unless there is a significant change in nutrient or chemical content or there is a potential health or safety risk for a population, such as allergic potential. However, there is considerable pressure on the government for mandatory labelling for genetically modified foods. For current information about volunteer labelling of food products resulting from genetic engineering or the regulations about these foods consult the web site for the Canadian Food Inspection Agency, Science Branch, Office of Biotechnology at http://www.inspection.gc.ca/english/sci/biotech/labeti/vole.shtml, or the Health Canada Food Program web site for Novel Foods and Ingredients at www.hc-sc.gc.ca/food-aliment/mh-dm/ofb-bba/nfi-ani/e_novel_foods_and_ingredient.html.

Nutrition Facts

The table with the title, Nutrition Facts, presents the nutrient content of a food, based on a specific amount of food in a standardized format on most prepackaged foods. All of the information in the Nutrition Facts table is based on a specific amount of food, a portion / serving. This portion / serving size is based on a reference amount of food, specified in the regulations and accessible in The Guide to Food

Labelling and Advertising[3]. The Nutrition Facts table lists Calories and the following 13 core food components / nutrients: Fat, Saturated fat, *trans* fat, cholesterol, sodium, carbohydrate, fiber, sugars, protein, vitamin A, vitamin C, calcium and iron. Other specified nutrients may be added to this list. For some nutrients the actual amount is given; for others the amount is expressed as % Daily Value. The % Daily Value gives a context to the actual amount of a nutrient, whether there is a lot or a little of a nutrient in the specific amount of food. (See 2.1 above)

Nutrient Content Claims

'Nutrient content claims' describe the relative amount of a nutrient in a food, whether it is "reduced" or "lower" in amount, or a "very high source." These claims must be consistent with the standards specified in the Guide to Food Labelling and Advertising[3].

Biological Role Claims

'Biological role claims' are claims that refer to the generally recognized nutritional function of energy or nutrients as an aid in maintaining the functions of the body for the maintenance of good health, or for normal growth and development. This type of claim is not new with these regulations. It should not be confused with a claim related to treating or preventing a specific disease.

Health-Related Claims

Health Canada has introduced new diet-related health claims, in addition to the permitted claims of the biological role of nutrients (above). Health claims are permitted about:
- potassium, sodium and reduced risk of high blood pressure;
- calcium, vitamin D and regular physical activity, and reduced risk of osteoporosis;
- saturated and *trans* fats and reduced risk of heart disease; and
- vegetables and fruit and reduced risk of some types of cancer.

Specific requirements related to the claims can be found in the Section VII: Health-Related Claims, Guide to Food Labelling and Advertising[3].

Educational Messages

The Nutrition Labelling Toolkit (available to health professionals and educators) focuses on four key messages to help consumers use the new nutrition labels:
- Nutrition Facts: Easy to find, easy to read, and on more foods.
- Use Nutrition Facts, the ingredient list and nutrition claims to make informed food choices.
- Nutrition Facts are based on a specific amount of food – compare this to the amount you eat.
- Use % Daily Value to see if a food has a 'lot' or a 'little' of a food component / nutrient relative to some other food item.

2.7 Food and Nutrition Surveillance in Canada

For an overview of what has and is being done regarding food and nutrition surveillance in Canada see http://www.hc-sc.gc.ca/fn-an/surveill/environmental_scan_table_e.html . Data sources include the recently released (July 2006) Canadian Community Health Survey - Nutrition (Cycle 2.2) http://www.statcan.ca/cgi-bin/imdb/p2SV.pl?Function=getSurvey&SDDS=5049&lang=en&db=IMDB&dbg=f&adm=8&dis=2 , recent provincial surveys and the Food Habits of Canadians survey [4]

References Cited

[1]. Regulations Amending the Food and Drug Regulations (Nutrition Labelling, Nutrient Content Claims and Health Claims). *Canadian Gazette Part II, Vol. 137, No. 1* pp.154-403. http://canadagazette.gc.ca/partII/2003/20030101/pdf/g2-13701.pdf

[2.] Beyond the Basics: Meal Planning for Healthy Eating, Diabetes Prevention and Management. Canadian Diabetes Association http://www.diabetes.ca/Section_Professionals/btb.asp (accessed July 05, 2006)

[3]. Canadian Food Inspection Agency. 2003 *Guide to Food Labelling and Advertising*. Ottawa. http://www.inspection.gc.ca/english/fssa/labeti/guide/toce.shtml.

[4] Gray-Donald K, Jacobs-Starkey L and Johnson-Down L. Food Habits of Canadians: Reduction in Fat Intake Over a Generation. Can Jour Publ Health 2000; 91 (5): 381-385 and Jacobs-Starkey L, Johnson-Down L and Gray-Donald K. Food Habits of Canadians: Comparison of Intakes in Adults and Adolescents to Canada's Food Guide to Healthy Eating. Can Jour Diet Prac Res 2001; 62 (2(: 61-69.

HIGHLIGHT 2 - A Vegetarian Diets

For Canada's rainbow Food Guide see **Figure 2.1** above. Also see, DC Position Statement: Vegetarian Food Guide for North America

http://www.dietitians.ca/news/highlights_positions.asp?fn=view&id=2515&idstring=5019%7C3941%7C3398%7C1231%7C2482%7C2175%7C2515%7C1952%7C2516%7C2517%7C1363%7C2451%7C1188%7C1338

Chapter 3 Canadian Information (Digestion, Absorption and Transport)

Alcohol does not require digestion and is quickly absorbed, especially on an empty stomach.

3-1 Alcohol Intake by Canadians, University Students and Recommendations for Alcohol Intake

During 2005, just under 80% of Canadians over 15 yrs consumed alcohol 44% of whom drink at least once a week (http://www.statcan.ca/english/ads/23F0001XCB/highlight.htm). Beer made up 80% of alcoholic beverages consumed by Canadians and has risen to the level of just over 80 liters per person over the age of 15 yrs. In addition, almost 14 liters of wine are consumed annually by these individuals as are 7.5 liters of spirits. Statistics Canada notes that these levels may be understated since they do not include home-made alcoholic beverages or those brewed-on-the-premises etc. It should also be noted that, over one in five (22.6%) of drinkers exceeded the low risk guidelines of, less than 14 drinks per week for males and 9 drinks per week for females, a behavior more common among those 18-24 yrs.

Alcohol consumption among Canadian university students: According to a Canadian Institutes for Health Research funded survey reported by Canada's Centre for Addiction and Mental Health (CAMH), a 2004 Canadian Campus Survey of over 6000 students from 40 universities revealed that 77% had consumed alcohol during the month prior to the study. Furthermore, 18.5 % and 6.6 % indicated that they consumed 5 or more or 8 or more drinks (binge drinking), respectively, on a single occasion once every 2 weeks or more frequently (http://www.camh.net/Research/Areas_of_research/Population_Life_Course_Studies/canadian_campus0 905.pdf). Also, almost one third of students reported at least one indicator of dependent drinking (e.g., being unable to stop). Males reported drinking more and higher amounts than females (8.9 vs 4.5 drinks per week) as well as reporting higher rates of episodic drinking, most of which occurred on weekends and off-campus but in private premises. In addition, almost one third of students reported at least one indicator of dependent drinking (e.g., being unable to stop). It should also be kept in mind that according to data from the Canadian Institutes of Health Information (CIHI), "that motor vehicle collisions were responsible for more than half (783) of the alcohol-related severe trauma hospitalizations in Canada in 2002–2003" (http://secure.cihi.ca/cihiweb/dispPage.jsp?cw_page=media_22jun2005_e).

For a brief but excellent review on alcohol and health see Rimm Eand Temple NJ. What Are the Health Implications of Alcohol Consumption ? in Temple NJ, Wilson T, Jacobs DR Jr (eds) Nutritional Health Strategies for Disease Prevention 2nd ed. Humana Press, New Jersey, 2006, pp 211 – 238. The *Nutrition Recommendations for Canadians* state that "The Canadian diet should include no more than 5% of total energy as alcohol, or two drinks daily, whichever is less"[1] and Health Canada also reminds Canadians that 'moderate drinking' is considered to be one drink or less per day and that more than four drinks on one occasion is a risk to health and safety [2]. The purpose of the recommendation was to limit alcohol intake, not to encourage alcohol consumption. The rationale for the recommendation is described on pp. 181-2 of Nutrition Recommendations[1]. See **bulleted text** and **illustration** on page 240 in the textbook for serving sizes of alcohol beverages that are considered one drink. It is especially important to note limiting alcohol intake in relation to pregnancy and fetal alcohol syndrome. Please refer to the Canadian Information Section in Chapter 13 of this supplement regarding Canada's recommendations for preventing fetal alcohol syndrome.

3-2 Legal Drinking Age in Canada

Unlike most states in the US where 'Legal Age' is 21 years old, in most provinces in Canada it is 19 (exceptions are Quebec, Alberta and Manitoba where it is 18)[3] and the blood alcohol limit is 0.08 per cent[4].

Canadian Readings:

- Centre for Addiction and Mental Health - http://www.camh.net/News_events/News_releases_and_media_advisories_and_backgrounders/canadian_campus_survey0905.html (accessed June 22, 2007)

- Canadian Center for Substance Abuse – http://www.ccsa.ca/ccsa (accessed June 25, 2007)

References Cited

[1]. Health and Welfare Canada. *Nutrition Recommendations.* Ottawa: Minister of Supply and Services Canada, 1990.

[2] Using the Food Guide handbook. Minister of Public Works and Government Services Canada, Ottawa 1997. http://www.hc-sc.gc.ca/fn-an/alt_formats/hpfb-dgpsa/pdf/food-guide-aliment/using_food_guide-servir_guide_alimentaire_e.pdf (accessed July 05, 2006)

[3] Legal Drinking Age by Province, In Canada. Canadian Center on Substance Abuse http://www.ccsa.ca/CCSA/EN/Topics/Legislation/LegalDrinkingAgeByProvCan.htm (accessed July 05, 2006)

[4] Road Safety in Canada – 2001. Transport Canada. http://www.tc.gc.ca/roadsafety/tp/tp13951/2001/page4.htm (accessed July 05, 2006)

Chapter 4 Canadian Information (Carbohydrates: Sugars, starches and fibers)

4-1 Carbohydrates are the primary sources of Energy for Adult Canadians

The primary source of Energy in the diet of Adult Canadians comes from Carbohydrates at 50% of Total Energy. (see Table 5 in the following weblink http://www.statcan.ca/english/research/82-620-MIE/82-620-MIE2006002.pdf). Further more, while their intake was steady from the mid-1970's to 1990 their level paralleled an increase in both total calories and fat from 1990 to 2000. How such increases relate to the rise in weight gain of both adults and children during this period remain to be fully explained (see Chapter 9). Recall from Chapter 2 that the DRI reports recommend a carbohydrate intake of 45 – 65 % of total calories but also that a maximum of 25 % of our calories come from added sugars. Note also that the Canadian Diabetes Association 2003 Clinical Practice Guidelines allows up to 10% of Total Energy as sugar (approximately 50 gr of sucrose per day in a 2000 kCal diet).

Indeed, based largely upon disappearance data, Statistics Canada estimates that, per capita, Canadians consumed 39.4 kg of sugar & syrup combine in 2001.[†] That would be like pouring more than 20 teaspoons of sugar onto / into your foods and beverages every day.

[†] Food Consumption in Canada Part II 2001 Statistics Canada Cat. No. 32-230 (http://www.statcan.ca/english/freepub/32-230-XIB/0000132-230-XIB.pdf)

Also, of particular interest to people with diabetes, the Canadian Food Inspection Agency and Health Canada recently clarified the requirements under the Food and Drug Regulations that pertain to the nutrient content descriptor "No Added Sugars" (see "Information Letter to Industry" http://www.inspection.gc.ca/english/fssa/labeti/nutrition/sugsuce.shtml), for example, if fruit juice / fruit juice concentrate are added to foods that otherwise would not contain them then this descriptor is not permitted.

4-2 Canadian Recommendations Concerning Intake of Carbohydrates

The Canadian recommendations concerning intake of carbohydrates are similar to those outlined in Chapter 4 of the textbook (e.g., margin of page 124). Other examples are shown below. Since the recommendations and guidelines are under revision, some of these may change. Check with the Health Canada web site for progress on the revisions (http://www.hc-sc.gc.ca/hpfb-dgpsa/onpp-bppn/revision_food_guide_e.html).

Eating Well with Canada's Food Guide
- Have vegetables and fruit more often than juice
- Make at least half of your grains whole grain each day

Carbohydrate Recommendations from the IOM DRI Report for young adult Canadians and Americans
- Acceptable Macro-nutrient Distribution Range (AMDR): 45 – 65 % of daily Calories
- RDA: 130 g (this value is based on the average minimum quantity of glucose used by the brain)
- Maximum amount of added sugars per day: 25 % of Total Calories

Reference Daily Values for Nutrition Facts Table
*   Carbohydrate – 300 g
*   Fibre – 25 g

Health Claim
*   A healthy diet rich in variety of fruits and vegetables may help reduce the risk of some types of cancer.

4-3 Fibre Content of Canadian Flour

The fibre content of flour in Canada varies from the values listed in **Appendix H, Table H1** of the textbook. In some cases the difference is significant. The values listed below in Table 4-1 are from *Nutrition Value of Some Common Foods*[1].

Table 4-1 Grams of Fibre in One Cup of Canadian Flour

Whole grain wheat, 16 g
Light rye, 15.7 g
Buckwheat, 4.4 g
All purpose wheat (white, enriched), 4.1 g
Cornmeal, 3.8 g
White rice flour, 3.6 g
Brown rice flour, 6.9 g

4-4 Diabetes in Canada

Diabetes is a growing problem in Canada, with more than 2 million people in Canada having diabetes[2]. The current estimated health care cost of diabetes in Canada as of 2004 is $13.2 billion every year. Funding for prevention and treatment of diabetes is a priority for federal and provincial governments. Programs include the Community Health Program for First Nations and Inuit (http://www.hc-sc.gc.ca/fnih-spni/pubs/home-domicile/prog_crit/index_e.html). The Canadian Diabetes Association (CDA) provides educational materials and programs for consumers and health professionals (www.diabetes.ca). The new address for the Canadian Diabetes Association is: 522 University Avenue, Suite 1400, Toronto, Ontario M5G 2R5.

As noted in **Section 2-4** above, the Canadian Diabetes Association recently announced the 'Beyond the Basics: Meal Planning for Healthy Eating, Diabetes Prevention and Management' poster[3] to help Canadians living with diabetes manage their carbohydrate intake. Although not currently used to counsel those with diabetes in the US, the CDA does advocate the use of the Glycemic Index (GI) during counselling[4]. It is used to help patients identify foods that are known to raise blood sugar to a lesser or greater degree than the reference food items, white bread or glucose, that are given a score of 100 (e.g., fruits such as apples have a 'low GI' and grains such as instant rice have a 'high GI' relative to reference standards). The concept of Glycemic Load (mathematical expression of GI of a food and its carbohydrate content i.e., GI of food x grams of carbohydrate in that food or meal) is also being explored in studies examining the effects of carbohydrates on blood sugar response (see **Glycemic Response** section and **Fig 4.13** in the textbook for more information and the Glycemic indices of selected foods, respectively).

Also, of particular interest to people with diabetes, the Canadian Food Inspection Agency and Health Canada recently clarified the requirements under the Food and Drug Regulations that pertain to the nutrient content descriptor "No Added Sugars" (see "Information Letter to Industry" http://www.inspection.gc.ca/english/fssa/labeti/nutrition/sugsuce.shtml), for example, if fruit juice / fruit juice concentrate are added to foods that otherwise would not contain them then this descriptor is not permitted.

References Cited

[1]. Health Canada. *Nutrient Value of Some Common Foods.* Ottawa: Canadian Government Publishing, 1999. www.hc-sc.gc.ca/food-aliment/ns-sc/nr-rn/surveillance/e_nutrient_value_of_some_common_.html (accessed June 25, 2007)

[2]. Canadian Diabetes Association. Diabetes Facts. www.diabetes.ca/Section_about/FactsIndex.asp. (accessed June 25, 2007)

[3] Canadian Diabetes Association. Beyond the Basics http://www.diabetes.ca/Section_Professionals/btb.asp (accessed June 25, 2007)

[4] Glycemic Index – the Index in Depth. http://www.diabetes.ca/Section_About/glycemic.asp (accessed June 25, 2007)

HIGHLIGHT 4 – Alternatives to Sugar

H4.1 Health Claim for Sugar Alcohols

The new nutrition labelling regulations permit a **health claim** for the role of sugar alcohols related to dental caries. The following claims would be acceptable[1].

- "Won't cause cavities."
- "Does not promote tooth decay."
- "Does not promote dental caries."
- "Non-cariogenic."
- "Tooth friendly. Won't cause cavities."
- "Tooth friendly. Does not promote tooth decay."
- "Tooth friendly. Does not promote dental caries."
- "Tooth friendly. Non-cariogenic."

In addition to many of the alternative sweeteners discussed in **Highlight 4** section of the textbook Health Canada recently approved Erythritol, a sugar alcohol similar to Xylitol for use in food items such as dietetic beverages and chewing gum[2].

References Cited

1. Regulations Amending the Food and Drug Regulations (Nutrition Labelling, Nutrient Content Claims and Health Claims). *Canadian Gazette Part II, Vol. 137, No. 1* pp.154-403.
   http://canadagazette.gc.ca/partII/2003/20030101/html/sor11-e.html (accessed June 25, 2007)

2. Canada Gazette II Vol 138 No. 25 - Dec 15, 2004, Regulations amending the Food and Drug Regulations (1242 – Erythritol).
   http://canadagazette.gc.ca/partII/2004/20041215/html/sor261-e.html (accessed June 25, 2007)

Chapter 5 Canadian Information ((The Lipids: Triglycerides, Phospholipids, and Sterols)

5-1 Canadian Recommendations Concerning Intake of Fats for Healthy People

The Canadian recommendations concerning intake of fats are similar to those in **Chapter 5** of the textbook (e.g., margin of page 160). They are listed below. Some of these, especially the Nutrition Recommendations for Canadians, will be changing to be consistent with the most recent IOM DRI reports[1].

Eating Well with Canada's Food Guide
- Vegetables and Fruit – Choose vegetables and fruit prepared with little or no added fat
- Vegetables and Fruit – Enjoy vegetables steamed, baked or stir-fried instead of deep fried
- Grain Products – Choose grain products that are low in fat
- Milk and Alternatives – Drink skim, 1%, or 2% milk each day
- Milk and Alternatives – Select lower fat milk alternatives
- Meat and Alternatives – Select lean meat and alternatives prepared with little or no added fat
- Meat and Alternatives - Trim visible fat from meats. Remove skin from poultry
- Meat and Alternatives - Use cooking methods such as roasting, baking or poaching that require little or no added fat
- Oils and Fats - Include 30-45 ml (2-3 Tbsp) of unsaturated fat each day
- Oils and Fats - Choose soft margarines that are low in saturated and trans fats
- Oils and Fats - Limit butter, hard margarine, lard and shortening

Reference Daily Values for the Nutrition Facts table on food labels (for a 2000 kCal diet)
- Fat – 65 g
- The sum of saturated fatty and *trans* fatty acids – 20 g

Nutrition Recommendations for young adult Canadians and Americans[1]
- AMDR: 20 – 35 % of Calories
- Omega-6 fatty acids 5 – 10 % of Calories and omega-3 fatty acids 0.6 – 1.2 %
- Levels of dietary Cholesterol, Saturated Fat and *trans* fat should be kept as low as possible while consuming a nutritionally adequate diet.
- Adequate Intake (AI) level of the omega-6 fatty acid is 12 g/day for females and 17 g/day for males.
- Adequate Intake (AI) level of the omega-3 fatty acid is 1.1 g/day for females and 1.6 g/day for males.

Health Claim
- A healthy diet low in saturated and *trans* fats may lower the risk of heart disease.

Recommendations of the 'Working Group on Hypercholesterolemia and Other Dyslipidemias' for the Management of Dyslipidemia and the Prevention of Cardiovascular Disease[2]
- Increase the proportion of mono- and poly-unsaturated fatty acids.
- Increase intake of omega-3 fatty acids.
- Decrease the proportion of saturated and *trans* fats to less than 7% of total calories.

5-2 Total fat intake and sources of fat for young adult Canadians

Data from the 2004 Canadian Community Health Survey 2.2 reveal that young adults (20-29 yrs) consume 31% of Total Energy from fat http://www.statcan.ca/english/research/82-620-MIE/82-620-MIE2006002.pdf it also revealed that for those over 19 years old (and using the names of the food groups from the previous Food Guide) that ~30% came from Meat and Alternatives, ~25% from fats & oils, chocolate bars, chips …, ~18% from Milk Products, ~15% from Grain Products and ~8% from Vegetables and Fruit .

5-3 Canadian Lipid Profile for Assessing Cardiovascular Disease (CVD) Risk

The Canadian Journal of Cardiology published the Canadian Cardiovascular Society position statement - Recommendations for the diagnosis and treatment of dyslipidemia and prevention of cardiovascular disease[2]. These recommendations do not provide single desirable blood lipid profile values similar to those shown in the textbook under risk factors for heart disease. Instead, the target values for the lipid components are listed according to the level of risk based on the patient's history. Using this approach, a person's risk for cardiovascular disease is assessed using more factors than the blood lipid profile, alone. For example, someone who has already been diagnosed with Type 2 Diabetes is considered at High risk for CVD.

5-4 *Trans* Fats in Canadian Foods

According to the new Canadian nutrition labelling regulations, the amount of *trans* fats in packaged foods is included together with saturated fats on the core list in the "Nutrition Facts" table on food labels. The amount is stated in grams and is included with saturated fat when calculating the %DV.

Most of the trans fats in the Canadian diet arise from the partially hydrogenated vegetable oils used to cook or make food items such as baked and fried foods. Trans fat not only raises plasma LDL-Cholesterol (bad cholesterol) it also reduces HDL-Cholesterol (good cholesterol). In the recently released (June 2006) final report of the Trans Fat Task Force (co-chaired by Health Canada and the Heart and Stroke Foundation of Canada) that was submitted to the Minister of Health, the Task Force agreed "to a regulatory approach to effectively eliminate trans fats in all processed foods or reduce it to the lowest possible level." (http://www.hc-sc.gc.ca/fn-an/nutrition/gras-trans-fats/tf-ge/tf-gt_rep-rap_e.html#ea). They also projected that if such action was taken that "the average daily intake of trans fats for all age groups would represent less than 1% of energy intake" a level consistent with recommendations from the World Health Organization and American Heart Association. Finally, in June 2007, Health Canada announced that it "is adopting the Trans Fat Task Force's recommendation on trans fats in Canadian foods, by calling on Canada's food industry to limit the trans fat content of vegetable oils and soft, spreadable margarines to 2 percent of the total fat content, and to limit the trans fat content for all other foods to 5 percent, including ingredients sold to restaurants" (http://www.hc-sc.gc.ca/ahc-asc/media/nr-cp/2007/2007_74_e.html). This announcement also revealed that the food industry will have two years to reduce the level of trans fat in foods the lowest levels possible by following the recommendations in the Trans Task Force Report and if significant progress is not made by that time regulations will be put in place to ensure target levels in the Report are met.

5-5 Fat in Canadian Ground Meats

The regulations about the fat in ground meat are different in Canada than in the U.S. (see below).

The Canadian Food Inspection Agency Guide to Food Labelling and Advertising[3] presents the following Canadian standards.

For Ground (naming the species) Meat Including Poultry Meat:

a) Composition:
"**Extra lean ground (naming the species)**" and "**lean ground (naming the species)**" are prescribed common names which may be used for ground meat, including poultry meat, containing no more than 10 percent fat and 17 percent fat, respectively.

b) Labelling:
The terms "**extra lean**" (no more than 10 percent fat), "**lean**" (no more than 17 percent fat), "**medium**" (no more than 23 percent fat) and "**regular**" (no more than 30 percent fat), are part of the prescribed common names for "**ground (naming the species)**" meat including poultry meat (S.94(4) and Schedule I, *Meat Inspection Regulations*).

5-6 Lower *trans* Vegetables oils

Vegetable oils are being improved, such that the finished product is lower in *trans* fatty acids. One such oil is an improved Canola oil[4] now available to restaurants, hospitals, foodservices and food manufacturers. They are being developed as an alternative for hydrogenated oils being used in these and other commercial operations.

5-7 Fat Replacers

Note: Fat replacers such as Simplesse, bean gums and fruit purees are found in Canadian food products, however, the fat replacer 'Olestra' (brand name, Olean) is not presently added to snack chips in Canada.

References Cited

1. Food and Nutrition Board, Institute of Medicine of the National Academies. Dietary Reference Intakes: Energy, Carbohydrate, Fiber, Fat, Fatty Acids, Cholesterol, Protein and Amino Acids. National Academies Press, Washington DC, 2002.

2. McPherson R, Frohlich J, Fodor G, Genest J. Canadian Cardiovascular Society position statement - Recommendations for the diagnosis and treatment of dyslipidemia and prevention of cardiovascular disease *Canadian Journal of Cardiology* 2006; 22 (11): 913-927. [For those with online access to Can J Cardiol [http://www.ccs.ca/download/position_statements/lipids.pdf] (accessed May 15, 2007)

3. Canadian Food Inspection Agency. 2003 *Guide to Food Labelling and Advertising*. Ottawa. http://www.inspection.gc.ca/english/fssa/labeti/guide/toce.shtml. (accessed June7, 2007)

4. Natreon Canola Oil. Dow AgroSciences   http://www.dowagro.com/natreon/canola/ (accessed June 05, 2007)

Chapter 6 Canadian Information (Protein: Amino Acids)

6-1 RDA & AMDR for Protein for young adult Canadians and Americans

RDA: 0.8 g/kg BW of good quality protein
AMDR: 10 – 35 % of Total Calories

Note: Protein Digestibility Corrected Amino Acid Scoring (PDCAAS) patterns for indispensable amino acids have also been proposed by the IOM for pre-school children and adults.

6-2 Protein intake by Canadian adults

The Canadian Community Health Survey of Canadians revealed that adults are obtaining about 17 % of their Total calories from protein.http://www.statcan.ca/english/research/82-620-MIE/82-620-MIE2006002.pdf (accessed June 26, 2007)

6-3 Protein and Amino Acid Supplements

Amino acid supplements (e.g., Arginine, Glutamine and Lysine) are not sold as food items in Canada but instead are regulated as Natural Health Products under the Natural Health Products Directorate of Health Canada. The new regulations for natural health products are in effect, with dates for required identification numbers and labelling extending as far ahead as 2009. Check the Natural Health Products Directorate web site at www.hc-sc.gc.ca/hpfb-dgpsa/nhpd-dpsn/index_e.html. The regulations can be found at http://www.hc-sc.gc.ca/dhp-mps/prodnatur/legislation/acts-lois/prodnatur/regs_cg2_e.html .

Caution is warranted when using any individual amino acid at levels much higher than those found in food. For example, Health Canada recently advised heart patients against the use of products containing L-arginine http://www.hc-sc.gc.ca/ahc-asc/media/advisories-avis/2006/2006_30_e.html

6-4 Protein Regulations for Canadian Food Labels

The nutrition labelling regulations in Canada identify a core requirement for the amount of protein in grams per serving of stated size for the Nutrition Facts table on food labels[1]. Unlike the case in the U.S., there is no DV set for protein on the new Canadian Nutrition Facts tables.

References Cited

[1]. Canada Gazette. Regulations Amending the Food and Drug Regulations (Nutrition Labelling, Nutrient Content Claims and Health Claims) December 2002. http://canadagazette.gc.ca/partII/2003/20030101/html/sor11-e.html (accessed July 07, 2006)

Chapter 7 Canadian Information (Metabolism: Transformations and Interactions)

HIGHLIGHT 7 – Alcohol and Nutrition

7-1 Canadian Recommendations on Alcohol Intake

The *Nutrition Recommendations for Canadians* state that "The Canadian diet should include no more than 5% of total energy as alcohol, or two drinks daily, whichever is less"[1] and Health Canada also reminds Canadians that 'moderate drinking' is considered to be one drink or less per day and that more than four drinks on one occasion is a risk to health and safety [2]. The purpose of the recommendation was to limit alcohol intake, not to encourage alcohol consumption. The rationale for the recommendation is described on pp. 181-2 of Nutrition Recommendations[1]. See **Bulleted text** PAGE 238 and **Figure** on page 239 and **Table H7.3** in the textbook for serving sizes of alcohol beverages that are considered one drink. It is especially important to note limiting alcohol intake in relation to pregnancy and fetal alcohol syndrome. Please refer to the Canadian Information Section in Chapter 15 of this CSI Doc regarding Canada's recommendations for preventing fetal alcohol syndrome.

7-2 Legal Drinking Age in Canada

Unlike most states in the US where 'Legal Age' is 21 years old, in most provinces in Canada it is 19 (exceptions are Quebec, Alberta and Manitoba where it is 18)[3] and the blood alcohol limit is 0.08 per cent[4] .

7-3 Alcohol consumption among Canadian university students

According to a Canadian Institutes for Health Research funded survey reported by Canada's Centre for Addiction and Mental Health (CAMH), a 2004 Canadian Campus Survey of over 6000 students from 40 universities revealed that 77% had consumed alcohol during the month prior to the study. Furthermore, 18.5 % and 6.6 % indicated that they consumed 5 or more or 8 or more drinks (binge drinking), respectively, on a single occasion once every 2 weeks or more frequently (http://www.camh.net/Research/Areas_of_research/Population_Life_Course_Studies/canadian_campus0 905.pdf). Also, almost one third of students reported at least one indicator of dependent drinking (e.g., being unable to stop). Males reported drinking more and higher amounts than females (8.9 vs 4.5 drinks per week) as well as reporting higher rates of episodic drinking, most of which occurred on weekends and off-campus but in private premises. In addition, almost one third of students reported at least one indicator of dependent drinking (e.g., being unable to stop). It should also be kept in mind that according to data from the Canadian Institutes of Health Information (CIHI), "that motor vehicle collisions were responsible for more than half (783) of the alcohol-related severe trauma hospitalizations in Canada in 2002–2003" (http://secure.cihi.ca/cihiweb/dispPage.jsp?cw_page=media_22jun2005_e).

For a brief but excellent review on alcohol and health see Rimm Eand Temple NJ. What Are the Health Implications of Alcohol Consumption ? in Temple NJ, Wilson T, Jacobs DR Jr (eds) Nutritional Health Strategies for Disease Prevention 2nd ed. Humana Press, New Jersey, 2006, pp 211 – 238.

Canadian Readings:

- Centre for Addiction and Mental Health -
http://www.camh.net/News_events/News_releases_and_media_advisories_and_backgrounders/canadian_campus_survey0905.html (accessed June 22, 2007)

- Canadian Center for Substance Abuse – http://www.ccsa.ca/ccsa (accessed June 22, 2007)

References Cited

[1]. Health and Welfare Canada. *Nutrition Recommendations.* Ottawa: Minister of Supply and Services Canada, 1990.

[2] Using the Food Guide handbook. Minister of Public Works and Government Services Canada, Ottawa 1997. http://www.hc-sc.gc.ca/fn-an/alt_formats/hpfb-dgpsa/pdf/food-guide-aliment/using_food_guide-servir_guide_alimentaire_e.pdf (accessed June 22, 2007)

[3] Legal Drinking Age by Province, In Canada. Canadian Center on Substance Abuse http://www.ccsa.ca/CCSA/EN/Topics/Legislation/LegalDrinkingAgeByProvCan.htm (accessed June 22, 2007)

[4] Road Safety in Canada – 2001. Transport Canada. http://www.tc.gc.ca/roadsafety/tp/tp13951/2001/page4.htm (accessed June 22, 2007)

Chapter 8 Canadian Information (Energy Balance and Body Composition)

8-1 Canadian Guidelines for Body Weight Classification in Adults

Health Canada published the Canadian Guidelines for Body Weight Classification in Adults in 2003, based on a technical report developed by Health Canada staff and an Expert Working Group of Canadian researchers[1]. The BMI ranges are similar to those in **Figure 8.6** in the textbook, but the Canadian Guidelines have slightly different descriptive terms. Table 8-2 below identifies the BMI categories and descriptors.

Table 8-1 Canadian BMI Categories and Levels of Health Risk[1]

BMI	Catergory	Level of Risk
<18.5	Underweight	Increased risk
18.5 – 24.9	Normal weight	Least risk
25.0 – 29.9	Overweight	Increased risk
30 and over	Obese	
30.0 – 34.9	Obese Class I	High risk
35.0 – 39.9	Obese Class II	Very high risk
≥40.0	Obese Class III	Extremely high risk

The guidelines also identify waist circumference as an important indicator of health risk. Increased risk of type 2 diabetes, coronary heart disease, and hypertension is associated with a waist circumference for[1]:
- men >102 cm (40 in.) and
- women >88 cm (35 in.)

The full report and a Quick Reference Tool for Professionals are available from the Health Canada web site http://www.hc-sc.gc.ca/fn-an/alt_formats/hpfb-dgpsa/pdf/nutrition/weight_book-livres_des_poids_e.pdf .

The '2006 Canadian clinical practice guidelines on the management and prevention of obesity in adults and children' which include recommendations to screen not only adults but also children and adolescents for overweight and obesity became available online in April 2007 (http://www.cmaj.ca/cgi/content/full/176/8/S1).

Note that the 'new' worldwide definition for Metabolic Syndrome (a cluster of the most dangerous heart attack risk factors: diabetes or prediabetes, abdominal obesity, changes in cholesterol and high blood pressure) recently announced by the International Diabetes Federation (IDF) (http://www.idf.org/home/index.cfm?unode=32EF2063-B966-468F-928C-A5682A4E3910) includes specific reference to abnormal abdominal fat distribution. According to the IDF "For a person to be defined as having the metabolic syndrome, the new definition requires they have central obesity, plus two of the following four additional factors: raised triglycerides, reduced HDL cholesterol, raised blood pressure, or raised fasting plasma glucose level."

---

[1]. Health Canada. Canadian Guidelines for Body Weight Classification in Adults. Ottawa: Health Canada

Publications Centre, 2003 http://www.hc-sc.gc.ca/fn-an/nutrition/weights-poids/cg_bwc_int-ld_cpa_int_e.html

HIGHLIGHT 8: Eating Disorders

The National Eating Disorder Centre in Toronto estimates that 200,000 to 300,000 women, aged 13 to 40 have anorexia nervosa, twice as many have bulimia (http://www.nedic.ca/MMWIP/b281a6a6793a4529/f19261a0cdcad338.shtml).

Both of the organizations below promote the non-diet approach to a healthy lifestyle:

- HUGS International offers support and programs for people seeking a lifestyle without dieting. The web site provides a self-profile quiz (www.hugs.com). HUGS International, Box 102A, R.R. #3, Portage la Prairie, Manitoba R1N 3A3 Phone: (204) 428-3432.

- The National Eating Disorder Information Centre (NEDIC) located in Toronto provides information through a toll-free phone number (1-866-633-4220) or (416) 340-4156 and the web site (www.nedic.ca). The website includes a guide for family and friends and numerous web-links to other Canadian (e.g., http://www.bana.ca/ and http://www.hopesgarden.org/), U.S. (e.g., http://www.nationaleatingdisorders.org/p.asp?WebPage_ID=337) and International (e.g., http://www.alda.org.ar/ and http://www.gurze.com/) websites dedicated to helping those with eating disorder issues.

For additional information and resources, you may wish to consult programs for eating disorders available at your college, university or community.

Chapter 9 Canadian Information (Weight Management: Overweight and Underweight)

9-1 Prevalence of Obesity in Canada

Health Canada has been monitoring the prevalence of overweight and obesity using data collected by the 1985 and 1990 Health Promotion Surveys, 1994, 1996 and 1998 Population Health Surveys and 2000 Canadian Community Health Survey[1]. Based on the results of the Canadian Community Health Survey, 15% of the population were obese in 2000-2001, a rate that has tripled in the past few decades[2]. The overweight- and obesity-related mortality rate has also increased in every province, with higher levels in Eastern Canada[1].

The first report of the Canadian Community Health Survey (2000/2001) presents statistics about the Body Mass Index (BMI) of Canadians from 1994/1995 to 2000/2001[3]. It should be noted that BMI values are for this period were based on self-reported height and weight. For children 7 to 13 years, the rate of obesity increased by 1.5 to 5 times between 1981 and 2001[4]. For example the rate of obesity among girls rose from 2% to 10% and for boys the rate of overweight rose from 9% to 20%.

More recent data from the Canadian Community Health Survey (2004) Cycle 2.2 using measured data revealed that for children 2-17 yrs, 18% were considered overweight and 8% were considered obese, a combined rate of 26% (http://www.statcan.ca/english/research/82-620-MIE/2005001/pdf/cobesity.pdf) . Table 9-1 below presents the Canadian proportions for adults for each BMI category, similar to those described in margin notes page 288 **Chapter 9** and in **Figure 8.7** in the textbook. Thus, more than half of the adult population in Canada is considered either overweight or obese.

Table 9-1 Proportion of Canadian Adults in each BMI Category (CCHS 2004)[3]

BMI Category	Proportion
Underweight (<18.5)	2%
Acceptable (18.5 – 24.9)	39%
Overweight (25.0 – 29.9)	36%
Obese (30 and over)	23%

9-2 Canadian Guidelines for Body Weight Classification in Adults

Health Canada published the Canadian Guidelines for Body Weight Classification in Adults in 2003, based on a technical report developed by Health Canada staff and an Expert Working Group of Canadian researchers[5]. The BMI ranges are similar those in **Figure 8.6** in the textbook, but the Canadian Guidelines have slightly different descriptive terms. Table 9-2 below identifies the BMI categories and descriptors.

Table 9-2 Canadian BMI Categories and Levels of Health Risk[4]

BMI	Catergory	Level of Risk
<18.5	Underweight	Increased risk
18.5 – 24.9	Normal weight	Least risk
25.0 – 29.9	Overweight	Increased risk
30 and over	Obese	
30.0 – 34.9	Obese Class I	High risk
35.0 – 39.9	Obese Class II	Very high risk
≥40.0	Obese Class III	Extremely high risk

The guidelines also identify waist circumference as an important indicator of health risk. Increased risk of type 2 diabetes, coronary heart disease, and hypertension is associated with a waist circumference for[5]:
- men >102 cm (40 in.) and
- women >88 cm (35 in.)

The full report and a Quick Reference Tool for Professionals are available from the Health Canada web site http://www.hc-sc.gc.ca/fn-an/alt_formats/hpfb-dgpsa/pdf/nutrition/weight_book-livres_des_poids_e.pdf .

The '2006 Canadian clinical practice guidelines on the management and prevention of obesity in adults and children' which include recommendations to screen not only adults but also children and adolescents for overweight and obesity became available online in April 2007 (http://www.cmaj.ca/cgi/content/full/176/8/S1).

Note: the 'new' worldwide definition for **Metabolic Syndrome** (a cluster of the most dangerous heart attack risk factors: diabetes or prediabetes, abdominal obesity, changes in cholesterol and high blood pressure) recently announced by the International Diabetes Federation (IDF) (http://www.idf.org/home/index.cfm?unode=32EF2063-B966-468F-928C-A5682A4E3910) includes specific reference to abnormal abdominal fat distribution. According to the IDF "For a person to be defined as having the metabolic syndrome, the new definition requires they have central obesity, plus two of the following four additional factors: raised triglycerides, reduced HDL cholesterol, raised blood pressure, or raised fasting plasma glucose level."

9-3 Herbal Products and Dietary Supplements Marketed for Weight Loss

Marketed weight-loss products, such as, ma huang (ephedra) and phenylpropanolamine are not legally available in Canada. You can check the Office of Natural Health Products web site (www.hc-sc.gc.ca/hpfb-dgpsa/nhpd-dpsn/index_e.html) to identify the status of herbs or natural products for which there are claims relating to weight loss. For over nine years now Health Canada has been advising Canadians about the risks associated with the use of products containing ephedrine http://www.hc-sc.gc.ca/ahc-asc/media/advisories-avis/2006/2006_33_e.html .

References Cited

[1]. P.T. Katzmarzyk and C.I. Arden, Overweight and obesity mortality trends in Canada, 1885-2000, *Canadian Journal of Public Health* 95 (2004): 16-20.

[2]. I. Strychar, Fighting obesity: A call to arms, *Canadian Journal of Public Health* 95 (2004): 12- 14.

[3]. Tjepkema M. 2005. Measured Obesity – Adult Obesity in Canada: Measured height and weight. http://www.statcan.ca/english/research/82-620-MIE/2005001/pdf/aobesity.pdf (accessed June 10, 2007)

[4]. Canadian Population Health Initiative. Improving the Health of Canadians: Summary Report. (accessed from
http://www.cihi.ca/cihiweb/dispPage.jsp?cw_page=PG_39_E&cw_topic=39&cw_rel=AR_322_E June 10, 2007).

[5]. Health Canada. Canadian Guidelines for Body Weight Classification in Adults. Ottawa: Health Canada Publications Centre, 2003 http://www.hc-sc.gc.ca/fn-an/nutrition/weights-poids/cg_bwc_int-ld_cpa_int_e.html

Highlight 9: Eating Disorders

Both of the organizations below promote the non-diet approach to a healthy lifestyle:

HUGS International offers support and programs for people seeking a lifestyle without dieting. The web site provides a self-profile quiz (www.hugs.com). HUGS International, Box 102A, R.R. #3, Portage la Prairie, Manitoba R1N 3A3 Phone: (204) 428-3432.

The National Eating Disorder Information Centre (NEDIC) located in Toronto provides information through a toll-free phone number (1-866-633-4220) or (416) 340-4156 and the web site (www.nedic.ca). The website includes a guide for family and friends and numerous web-links to other Canadian (e.g., http://www.bana.ca/ and http://www.hopesgarden.org/), U.S. (e.g., http://www.nationaleatingdisorders.org/p.asp?WebPage_ID=337) and International (e.g., http://www.alda.org.ar/ and http://www.gurze.com/) websites dedicated to helping those with eating disorder issues.

For additional information and resources, you may wish to consult programs for eating disorders available at your college, university or community.

Chapter 10 Canadian Information (The Water Soluble Vitamins: B Vitamins and Vitamin C)

10-1 Nutrient Enrichment of Foods Sold in Canada

Canadian students should be aware of the current Canadian policies about nutrient enrichment of foods. These policies differ from those in the United States and thus the vitamin and mineral content of some Canadian foods may differ from the food sources of nutrients listed in the text. This may also affect the results of nutrient analysis of student food intakes. The Canadian *Food and Drug Regulations*[1] specify the foods to which nutrients may or must be added, and the amounts which may be added. Canadian regulations are sometimes more restrictive and thus many Canadian foods have lower amounts of some vitamins and minerals. Bleached wheat flour is one of the staple foods for which it is mandatory to add back nutrients that were lost during processing and also serve as a vehicle to increase the folic acid level of the Canadian diet. The nutrients that must be added are thiamine, riboflavin, niacin, iron and folic acid.

Nutrient values from food composition tables and computerized nutrient analysis programs based on United States data, such as that found in **Appendix H** in the textbook and the *Diet Analysis* software that may accompany your text, do not accurately reflect Canadian foods and nutrient intakes. Breakfast cereals are common examples of this variation. This is especially true for vitamins A and D which can be higher in the United States cereal products. Vitamins A and D are presently not permitted to be added to cereals in Canada. Annex 2, Section VI in Guide to Food Labelling and Advertising[2] provides detailed information about foods to which nutrients can be added. *Nutrient Value of Some Common Foods* was revised and published by Health Canada in 1999. It is a quick reference for Canadian foods using the 1997 Canadian Nutrient Data File[3] . The 2007b edition of the Canadian Nutrient File is now available electronically. It now contains 5370 food items and can be searched on-line at http://www.hc-sc.gc.ca/fn-an/nutrition/fiche-nutri-data/index_e.html . As part of the search one can also find out what constitutes a serving according to CFGHE for food items such as milk (e.g., 250 ml of milk = 1 serving; a medium size apple = 1 serving) . If interested, one can also drill down to find the Energy content and Macro- & Micro-nutrient content of each food item, as well.

The review of Canadian regulations about the addition of vitamins and minerals to foods that began in January 1998 is now complete and Health Canada's proposed policy and implementation plans can be viewed at http://www.hc-sc.gc.ca/fn-an/nutrition/vitamin/fortification_factsheet2-fiche2_e.html . Some of the reasons for this review were to maintain and improve the food supply, protect Canadians from health hazards due to nutrient excesses and prevent misleading practices.

10-2 Canadian Daily Values for Vitamins

Some of the Canadian Reference Daily Values for vitamins are different from those listed in the textbook and are based on the Recommended Daily Intake for vitamins[2.] The daily values for vitamins for persons 2 years of age and older are listed in Table 10-1 of this CSI Document. When you look at the vitamin-specific Figures in the textbook that provide examples of the sources of the different vitamins, you might want to compare the amount in foods to the Canadian Reference Daily Values list below.

Table 10-1 Daily Values for Vitamins in Canada for Persons 2 Years and Older, Compared to U.S. DV

Vitamin	Daily Value (RDI)[a]	U.S. Daily Value
Vitamin A	1000 RE	5000 IU[b]
Vitamin D	5 µg	400 IU[c]
Vitamin E	10 mg	30 IU[d]
Vitamin K	80 µg	80 ug
Thiamin	1.3 mg	1.5 mg
Riboflavin	1.6 mg	1.7 mg
Niacin	23 mg	20 mg
Folate	220 µg	400 ug
Vitamin B$_{12}$	2 µg	6 ug
Vitamin B$_6$	1.8 mg	2 mg
Vitamin C	60 mg	60 mg
Biotin	30 ug	300 ug
Pantothenic acid	7 mg	10 mg

[a] Regulations Amending the Food and Drug Regulations (Nutrition Labelling, Nutrient Content Claims and Health Claims). *Canadian Gazette Part II, Vol. 137, No. 1* pp.154-403. http://gazetteducanada.gc.ca/partII/2003/20030101/html/sor11-e.html (accessed June 10, 2007)

[b] multiply by 0.3 to convert to retinol
[c] divide by 40 to convert to ug
[d] divide by 1.5 to convert to mg

References Cited

[1]. Health and Welfare Canada. *Departmental Consolidation of the Food and Drugs Act and Regulations.* Ottawa: Ministry of Supply and Services, 2001. The current regulations can be found at http://www.hc-sc.gc.ca/fn-an/legislation/acts-lois/fdr-rad/index_e.html   (accessed June 05, 2007)

[2]. Canadian Food Inspection Agency. 2003 *Guide to Food Labelling and Advertising.* Ottawa. http://www.inspection.gc.ca/english/fssa/labeti/guide/toce.shtml. (accessed June 05, 2007)

[3] Health Canada. *Nutrient Value of Some Common Foods.* Ottawa: Public Works and Government Services Canada, 1999. www.hc-sc.gc.ca/food-aliment/ns-sc/nr-rn/surveillance/e_nutrient_value_of_some_common_.html (accessed June 05, 2007)

Highlight 10 – Vitamin and Mineral Supplements

H10.1 Canadian Regulation of Supplements

Vitamin and mineral supplements that are considered drugs are regulated in Canada under Part D of the Food and Drugs Act and Regulations[1]. The regulations set minimum and maximum levels for vitamins in supplements. At higher doses, some such as vitamin K, can be sold only by prescription. Regulations control advertising of supplements, preventing recommendations of high doses of nutrients.

Non-prescription single and multiple vitamin mineral supplements (including those from natural sources) are regulated under the Natural Health Products Directorate of Health Canada. The new regulations for natural health products are in effect. Fifty seven per cent of Canadians recently reported taking Vitamins (http://www.hc-sc.gc.ca/dhp-mps/pubs/natur/eng_cons_survey_e.html). Check for updates on Natural Health Products Directorate at www.hc-sc.gc.ca/hpfb-dgpsa/nhpd-dpsn/index_e.html. The Natural Health Product Regulations can be found at http://www.hc-sc.gc.ca/dhp-mps/prodnatur/legislation/acts-lois/prodnatur/index_e.html .

If you are a Canadian student living near the United States border, you may find it interesting to compare the cost and the content of vitamin and mineral supplements from each country. You will also notice that U.S. vitamin / mineral supplements have a **Supplement Facts** panel on them that includes the quantity of each nutrient listed in it along with their respective %DV (see **Figure H10.1** in the textbook) while ours does not provide a %DV for each nutrient.

Eating Well with Canada's Food Guide now recommends that "All women who could become pregnant and those who are pregnant or breastfeeding need a multivitamin containing **folic acid** every day" http://www.hc-sc.gc.ca/fn-an/alt_formats/hpfb-dgpsa/pdf/food-guide-aliment/print_eatwell_bienmang_e.pdf .

References Cited

[1] Health and Welfare Canada. *Departmental Consolidation of the Food and Drugs Act and Regulations.* Ottawa: Ministry of Supply and Services, 2001. The current regulations can be found at at http://www.hc-sc.gc.ca/fn-an/legislation/acts-lois/fda-lad/index_e.html (accessed June 05, 2007)

Chapter 11 Canadian Information (The Fat Soluble Vitamins: A, D, E, and K)

11-1 Nutrient Enrichment of Foods Sold in Canada

Canadian students should be aware of the current Canadian policies about nutrient enrichment of foods. These policies differ from those in the United States and thus the vitamin and mineral content of some Canadian foods may differ from the food sources of nutrients listed in the text. This may also affect the results of nutrient analysis of student food intakes. The Canadian *Food and Drug Regulations*[1] specify the foods to which nutrients may or must be added, and the amounts which may be added. Canadian regulations are sometimes more restrictive and thus many Canadian foods have lower amounts of some vitamins and minerals. Bleached wheat flour is one of the staple foods for which it is mandatory to add back nutrients that were lost during processing and also serve as a vehicle to increase the folic acid level of the Canadian diet. The nutrients that must be added are thiamine, riboflavin, niacin, iron and folic acid.

Nutrient values from food composition tables and computerized nutrient analysis programs based on United States data, such as that found in **Appendix H** in the textbook and the *Diet Analysis* software that may accompany your text, do not accurately reflect Canadian foods and nutrient intakes. Breakfast cereals are common examples of this variation. This is especially true for vitamins A and D which can be higher in the United States cereal products. Vitamins A and D are presently not permitted to be added to cereals in Canada. Annex 2, Section VI in Guide to Food Labelling and Advertising[2] provides detailed information about foods to which nutrients can be added. *Nutrient Value of Some Common Foods* was revised and published by Health Canada in 1999. It is a quick reference for Canadian foods using the 1997 Canadian Nutrient Data File[3] . The 2007b edition of the Canadian Nutrient File is now available electronically. It now contains 5370 food items and can be searched on-line at http://www.hc-sc.gc.ca/fn-an/nutrition/fiche-nutri-data/index_e.html . As part of the search one can also find out what constitutes a serving according to CFGHE for food items such as milk (e.g., 250 ml of milk = 1 serving; a medium size apple = 1 serving). If interested, one can also drill down to find the Energy content and Macro- & Micro-nutrient content of each food item, as well.

The review of Canadian regulations about the addition of vitamins and minerals to foods that began in January 1998 is now complete and Health Canada's proposed policy and implementation plans can be viewed at http://www.hc-sc.gc.ca/fn-an/nutrition/vitamin/fortification_factsheet2-fiche2_e.html . Some of the reasons for this review were to maintain and improve the food supply, protect Canadians from health hazards due to nutrient excesses and prevent misleading practices.

11-2 Canadian Daily Values for Vitamins

Some of the Canadian Reference Daily Values for vitamins are different from those listed in the textbook and are based on the Recommended Daily Intake for vitamins[4]. The daily values for vitamins for persons 2 years of age and older are listed in Table 11-1 of this CSI Document. When you look at the vitamin-specific Figures in the textbook that provide examples of the sources of the different vitamins, you might want to compare the amount in foods to the Canadian Reference Daily Values list below.

Table 11-1 Daily Values for Vitamins in Canada for Persons 2 Years and Older, Compared to U.S. DV

Vitamin	Daily Value (RDI)[a]	U.S. Daily Value
Vitamin A	1000 RE	5000 IU[b]
Vitamin D	5 µg	400 IU[c]
Vitamin E	10 mg	30 IU[d]
Vitamin K	80 µg	80 ug
Thiamin	1.3 mg	1.5 mg
Riboflavin	1.6 mg	1.7 mg
Niacin	23 mg	20 mg
Folate	220 µg	400 ug
Vitamin B_{12}	2 µg	6 ug
Vitamin B_6	1.8 mg	2 mg
Vitamin C	60 mg	60 mg
Biotin	30 ug	300 ug
Pantothenic acid	7 mg	10 mg

[a] Regulations Amending the Food and Drug Regulations (Nutrition Labelling, Nutrient Content Claims and Health Claims). *Canadian Gazette Part II, Vol. 137, No. 1* pp.154-403.
http://gazetteducanada.gc.ca/partII/2003/20030101/html/sor11-e.html (accessed June 06, 2007)

[b] multiply by 0.3 to convert to retinol

[c] divide by 40 to convert to ug

[d] divide by 1.5 to convert to mg

11-3 An example of a Health Claim on Canadian Food Labels that includes Vitamin D:
" A healthy diet with adequate calcium and vitamin D, and regular physical activity, help to achieve strong bones and may reduce the risk of osteoporosis."[4]

References Cited

[1]. Health and Welfare Canada. *Departmental Consolidation of the Food and Drugs Act and Regulations.* Ottawa: Ministry of Supply and Services, 2001. The current regulations can be found at http://www.hc-sc.gc.ca/fn-an/legislation/acts-lois/fdr-rad/index_e.html (accessed June 05, 2007)

[2]. Canadian Food Inspection Agency. 2003 *Guide to Food Labelling and Advertising.* Ottawa. http://www.inspection.gc.ca/english/fssa/labeti/guide/toce.shtml. (accessed June 05, 2007)

[3] Health Canada. *Nutrient Value of Some Common Foods.* Ottawa: Public Works and Government Services Canada, 1999. www.hc-sc.gc.ca/food-aliment/ns-sc/nr-rn/surveillance/e_nutrient_value_of_some_common_.html (accessed June 05, 2007)

[4]. Regulations Amending the Food and Drug Regulations (Nutrition Labelling, Nutrient Content Claims and Health Claims). *Canadian Gazette Part II, Vol. 137, No. 1* pp.154-403. http://gazetteducanada.gc.ca/partII/2003/20030101/html/sor11-e.html (accessed June 05, 2007)

Highlight 11 – Antioxidant Nutrients in Disease Prevention

H11.1 Safety of Some Supplements ?

Health Canada recently published (January 2006) information about the safety of Vitamin E supplements http://www.hc-sc.gc.ca/iyh-vsv/alt_formats/cmcd-dcmc/pdf/vitam_e.pdf , information that suggests that at high doses it may increase the risk of heart disease in those who are at high risk for heart disease.

Vitamin and mineral supplements that are considered drugs are regulated in Canada under Part D of the Food and Drugs Act and Regulations[1]. The regulations set minimum and maximum levels for vitamins in supplements. At higher doses, some such as Vitamin K, can be sold only by prescription. Regulations control advertising of supplements, preventing recommendations of high doses of nutrients.

Non-prescription single and multiple vitamin mineral supplements (including those from natural sources) are regulated under the Natural Health Products Directorate of Health Canada. The new regulations for natural health products are in effect. Fifty seven per cent of Canadians recently reported taking Vitamins (http://www.hc-sc.gc.ca/dhp-mps/pubs/natur/eng_cons_survey_e.html). Check for up-dates on Natural Health Products Directorate at   www.hc-sc.gc.ca/hpfb-dgpsa/nhpd-dpsn/index_e.html. The Natural Health Product Regulations can be found at http://www.hc-sc.gc.ca/dhp-mps/prodnatur/legislation/acts-lois/prodnatur/index_e.html . If you are a Canadian student living near the United States border, you may find it interesting to compare the cost and the content of vitamin and mineral supplements from each country. You will also notice that U.S. vitamin / mineral supplements have a **Supplement Facts** panel on them that includes the quantity of each nutrient listed in it along with their respective %DV (see **Figure H10.1** in the textbook) while ours does not provide a %DV for each nutrient.

References Cited

[1] Health and Welfare Canada. *Departmental Consolidation of the Food and Drugs Act and Regulations.* Ottawa: Ministry of Supply and Services, 2001. The current regulations can be found at http://www.hc-sc.gc.ca/fn-an/legislation/acts-lois/fdr-rad/index_e.html (accessed July 05, 2006)

Chapter 12 Canadian Information (Water and Major Minerals)

12-1 Water Quality in Canada

Water quality is an important issue in Canada, where a number of deaths have been caused by unsafe water supplies. Health and environmental departments of the federal, provincial and territorial governments have responsibilities related to safe water. Health Canada has a web site that reports on water quality activities (http://www.hc-sc.gc.ca/ewh-semt/water-eau/index_e.html).

12-2 Bottled Water in Canada

You can find information about the bottled water in Canada by referring to a fact sheet from the Canadian Food Inspection Agency, "Food Safety Facts on Bottled Water," available at http://www.inspection.gc.ca/english/fssa/concen/specif/bottwate.shtml.

Note: New regulations for Bottled Water are in the final stage of consultation (see http://www.hc-sc.gc.ca/fn-an/consultation/init/bottle_water-eau_embouteillee_tc-tm_e.html) and are expected to be published in Canada Gazette I or II by the end of 2007.

12-3 Canadian Daily Values for Minerals

Aside from those for sodium and potassium, the Canadian reference DV's for minerals that are used to indicate the %DV for minerals in Nutrition Facts tables on foods are different from those listed in the textbook and are based, in part, on the Recommended Daily Intake for minerals[1]. The daily values for the major minerals for persons 2 years of age and older are listed in Table 12-1 of this CSI Document. In fact, currently, only some, such as, sodium, potassium and chloride have the same DV in Canada and the United States. The differences in daily values may be important if you are using % DV in foods to assess mineral intake.

Table 12-1 Daily Values for Minerals in Canada for Persons 2 Years and Older[1], Compared to United States DV

Mineral	Canadian Daily Value (RDI)	United States Daily Value
Calcium	1100 mg	1000 mg
Phosphorus	1100 mg	1000 mg
Magnesium	250 mg	400 mg
Sodium	2400 mg	2400 mg
Potassium	3500 mg	3500 mg
Iron	14 mg	18 mg
Zinc	9 mg	15 mg
Iodide	160 µg	150 µg
Selenium	50 ug	70 ug
Copper	2 mg	2 mg
Manganese	2 mg	2 mg
Chromium	120 ug	120 ug
Molybdenum	75 ug	75 ug
Chloride	3400 mg	3400 mg

12-4 Calcium in Canadian Foods

Canadian regulations for adding calcium to foods and beverages (fortification) differ from those in the United States. Some milk products, such as fluid milk or milk substitutes, contain added milk solids, thus increasing the amount of calcium in milk by up to 33%. Some fruit juice products, such as orange juice, have added milk solids or added calcium. These are often sold as calcium supplements. You should read the labels of these products carefully to compare calcium content and cost.

Consider this: What is the Vitamin D intake or status of those using non-milk products as major sources of calcium ?

Also, keep in mind that the new Nutrition Labelling regulations not only include calcium among the core nutrients or food components that must be listed in the Nutrition Facts table and that Health Canada recently allowed food manufacturers to use a **diet-related heath claim** on foods meeting certain criteria, linking calcium, vitamin D and physical activity with osteoporosis but, as with all other diet-related health claims, the exact wording is prescribed. One example of such a claim is "A healthy diet with adequate calcium and vitamin D, and regular physical activity, help to achieve strong bones and may reduce the risk of osteoporosis". In addition, the Natural Health Products Directorate allows biological role / structure function claims on vitamin and mineral supplements that contain those nutrients at levels at or above the RDA / AI, for example, for calcium "Helps to prevent bone resorption and osteoporosis" (http://www.hc-sc.gc.ca/dhp-mps/prodnatur/applications/licen-prod/monograph/mono_calcium_e.html).

12-5 Canadian Salt and Sodium Intake Guidelines

Eating Well with Canada's Food Guide[†] recommends
- Vegetable and Fruit – Choose vegetables and fruit prepared with little or no added fat, sugar or salt.
- Grain Products – Choose grain products that are lower in fat, sugar or salt.
- Meat and Alternatives – Select lean meat and alternatives prepared with little or no added fat or salt.
- Meat and Alternatives – If you eat luncheon meats, sausages or prepackaged meats, choose those lower in salt (sodium) and fat.
- Eat Well – Limiting foods and beverages high in … salt (sodium) such as … potato chips, nachos and other salty snacks … .
- Read the label – Compare the Nutrition Facts table on food labels to choose products that contain less … and sodium.

[†](http://www.hc-sc.gc.ca/fn-an/food-guide-aliment/ordercommander/eating_well_bien_manger_e.html)

12-6 Canadian Salt (Sodium) Intake

Even with the exclusion of salt added at the table or while cooking, the usual intake of sodium by the vast majority of adults (19-70 yrs) not only exceed the AI for sodium (1300 – 1500 mg/day) they also exceed the UL (2300 mg/day) as well, a level beyond which health risk increases, however, it should be noted that females do consume significantly less than their male counterparts (http://www.statcan.ca/english/freepub/82-003-XIE/2006004/articles/sodium/findings.htm). Also, the food grouping that contributed the greatest amount of sodium to the diet (~ 20%) was 'pizza, sandwiches, submarines, hamburgers and hotdogs' followed by 'soups' at ~ 7 %.

12-7 Sodium and Potassium on Canadian Labels

Sodium is a core nutrient on all Nutrition Facts labels with the amount expressed in both milligrams and as % DV[1], under the new Nutrition Labelling Regulations. Potassium is not a core nutrient. However, potassium content must be declared if the pre-packaged food contains added potassium salts or if there is any claim or advertisement about the absence or reduced level of salt or sodium in the food. In these cases the amount of potassium is stated in both milligrams and as a % DV. For example, 'Salt-Free' or 'Sodium-Free' means less than 5 mg of sodium is present in the amount or serving of a stated size (these reference amounts or servings are regulated by Health Canada). Also, foods with < 5% DV would not be considered high in sodium.

The new labelling regulations also allow a health claim linking sodium and potassium to high blood pressure[1]. The regulations provide prescribed wording of the claim. Potassium content must appear on the Nutrition Facts table when such a claim is made.

Example of a **Diet-related Health Claim**: "A healthy diet containing foods high in potassium and low in sodium may reduce the risk of high blood pressure, a risk factor for stroke and heart disease."[1]

References Cited

[1]. Regulations Amending the Food and Drug Regulations (Nutrition Labelling, Nutrient Content Claims and Health Claims). *Canada Gazette Part II, Vol. 137, No. 1* pp.154-403.
http://canadagazette.gc.ca/partII/2003/20030101/html/sor11-e.html (accessed June 6, 2007)

HIGHLIGHT 12: Osteoporosis and Calcium

H12-1 Canadian Osteoporosis Society's approach to prevention, diagnosis and management of osteoporosis:

See summary of the 2002 evidence-based guidelines for Osteoporosis, the first of their kind in the world (http://www.osteoporosis.ca/english/News/GuidelinesNewsRelease/). This site also includes access to the full report published in a Supplement to a recent issue of the Canadian Medical Association Journal (see reference under Canadian Reading below).

H12-2 Calcium on food labels:

The new Nutrition Labelling regulations not only include calcium among the core nutrients or food components that must be listed in the Nutrition Facts table but also permit a Health Claim about calcium and vitamin D and physical activity and a link to osteoporosis[1]. The regulations prescribe the wording for such a claim.

Example of a **Diet-Related Health Claim** for a link between calcium and osteoporosis: "A healthy diet with adequate calcium and vitamin D, and regular physical activity, help to achieve strong bones and may reduce the risk of osteoporosis."[1]

Canadian Reading
Brown JP, Josse RG and The Scientific Advisory Council of the Osteoporosis Society of Canada. 2002 clinical practice guidelines for the diagnosis and management of osteoporosis in Canada. *Canadian Medical Association Journal* 167 (10 Suppl)(2002): 1S.

References Cited
[1]. Regulations Amending the Food and Drug Regulations (Nutrition Labelling, Nutrient Content Claims and Health Claims). *Canadian Gazette Part II, Vol. 137, No. 1* pp.154-403.
http://canadagazette.gc.ca/partII/2003/20030101/html/sor11-e.html (accessed June 6, 2007)

Chapter 13 Canadian Information (Trace Minerals)

13-1 Canadian Daily Values for Minerals

Aside from those for sodium and potassium, the Canadian reference DV's for minerals that are used to indicate the %DV for minerals in Nutrition Facts tables on foods are different from those listed in the textbook and are based, in part, on the Recommended Daily Intake for minerals[1]. The daily values for the major and trace minerals for persons 2 years of age and older are listed in Table 13-1 of this CSI Document. In fact, currently, only some, such as, sodium, potassium and chloride have the same DV in Canada and the United States and those for iron and zinc are lower than U.S. reference values. The differences in daily values may be important if you are using % DV in foods to assess mineral, especially iron, intake.

Table 13-1 Daily Values for Minerals in Canada for Persons 2 Years and Older[1], Compared to United States DV

Mineral	Canadian Daily Value (RDI)	United States Daily Value
Calcium	1100 mg	1000 mg
Phosphorus	1100 mg	1000 mg
Magnesium	250 mg	400 mg
Sodium	2400 mg	2400 mg
Potassium	3500 mg	3500 mg
Iron	14 mg	18 mg
Zinc	9 mg	15 mg
Iodide[a]	160 µg	150 µg
Selenium	50 ug	70 ug
Copper	2 mg	2 mg
Manganese	2 mg	2 mg
Chromium	120 ug	120 ug
Molybdenum	75 ug	75 ug
Chloride	3400 mg	3400 mg

[a] In Canada the Food and Drug Regulations, Division 17 (**B.17.003.**), stipulates that "Notwithstanding section B.17.001, salt for table or general household use shall contain 0.01 per cent potassium iodide ..." (http://www.hc-sc.gc.ca/fn-an/alt_formats/hpfb-dgpsa/pdf/legislation/e_d-text-2.pdf)

13-2 Nutrient Enrichment of Foods Sold in Canada

Canadian students should be aware of the current Canadian policies about nutrient enrichment of foods. These policies differ from those in the United States and thus the vitamin and mineral content of some Canadian foods may differ from the food sources of nutrients listed in the text. This may also affect the results of nutrient analysis of student food intakes. The Canadian *Food and Drug Regulations*[2] specify the foods to which nutrients may or must be added, and the amounts which may be added. Canadian regulations are sometimes more restrictive and thus many Canadian foods have lower amounts of some vitamins and minerals. Bleached wheat flour is one of the staple foods for which it is mandatory to add back nutrients that were lost during processing and also serve as a vehicle to increase the folic acid level of the Canadian diet. The nutrients that must be added are thiamine, riboflavin, niacin, **iron** and folic acid.

Note: Iron is one of the 13 food components that are now mandatory on the **Nutrition Facts** table on most pre-packaged foods sold in Canada and the U.S..

Nutrient values from food composition tables and computerized nutrient analysis programs based on United States data, such as **Appendix H** in the textbook and the *Diet Analysis Plus* software, do not accurately reflect Canadian foods and nutrient intakes. Breakfast cereals are common examples of this variation. This is especially true for vitamins A and D which can be higher in the United States cereal products. Vitamins A and D are presently not permitted to be added to cereals in Canada. Annex 2, Section VI in Guide to Food Labelling and Advertising[3] provides detailed information about foods to which nutrients can be added. *Nutrient Value of Some Common Foods* was revised and published by Health Canada in 1999. It is a quick reference for Canadian foods using the 1997 Canadian Nutrient Data File[4] The 2007b edition of the Canadian Nutrient File is now available electronically. It now contains 5370 food items and can be searched on-line at http://www.hc-sc.gc.ca/fn-an/nutrition/fiche-nutri-data/index_e.html . As part of the search one can also find out what constitutes a serving according to CFGHE for food items such as milk (e.g., 250 ml of milk = 1 serving; a medium size apple = 1 serving) . If interested, one can also drill down to find the Energy content and Macro- & Micro-nutrient content of each food item, as well.

The review of Canadian regulations about the addition of vitamins and minerals to foods that began in January 1998 is now complete and Health Canada's proposed policy and implementation plans can be viewed at http://www.hc-sc.gc.ca/fn-an/nutrition/vitamin/fortification_factsheet2-fiche2_e.html . Some of the reasons for this review were to maintain and improve the food supply, protect Canadians from health hazards due to nutrient excesses and prevent misleading practices.

References Cited

[1]. Health and Welfare Canada. *Departmental Consolidation of the Food and Drugs Act and Regulations*. Ottawa: Ministry of Supply and Services, 2001. The current regulations can be found at http://www.hc-sc.gc.ca/fn-an/legislation/acts-lois/fdr-rad/index_e.html (accessed June 05, 2007)

[2]. Canadian Food Inspection Agency. 2003 *Guide to Food Labelling and Advertising*. Ottawa. http://www.inspection.gc.ca/english/fssa/labeti/guide/toce.shtml. (accessed June 05, 2007)

[3] Health Canada. *Nutrient Value of Some Common Foods.* Ottawa: Public Works and Government Services Canada, 1999. www.hc-sc.gc.ca/food-aliment/ns-sc/nr-rn/surveillance/e_nutrient_value_of_some_common_.html (accessed June 05, 2007)

[4]. Regulations Amending the Food and Drug Regulations (Nutrition Labelling, Nutrient Content Claims and Health Claims). *Canadian Gazette Part II, Vol. 137, No. 1* pp.154-403. http://gazetteducanada.gc.ca/partII/2003/20030101/html/sor11-e.html (accessed June 05, 2007)

HIGHLIGHT 13 – Phytochemicals and Functional Foods

What Do They Promise? What Do They Deliver?

Canadian regulations for health claims on labels for foods and natural health products and for advertising are different from those in the United States. Many of the claims related to phytochemicals and functional foods apply more to natural health products. Check the following web sites for the most current information about product specific claims. Sources of information about the regulations are:

- Health claims for foods - http://canadagazette.gc.ca/partII/2003/20030101/html/sor11-e.html
- Natural Health Products – http://www.hc-sc.gc.ca/hpfb-dgpsa/nhpd-dpsn/index_e.html
- Canadian Code of Advertising Standards –
     http://www.adstandards.com/en/Standards/adStandards.pdf
- Functional foods and nutraceuticals – http://www.hc-sc.gc.ca/fn-an/label-etiquet/nutrition/claims-reclam/nutra-funct_foods-nutra-fonct_aliment_e.html

For examples of some of the terms used to define / describe phytochemicals and functional foods and some specific examples of their possible effects and food sources see the Glossary on page 469, **Table H13.1** along with **Figure H13.1** in the textbook.

Chapter 14 Canadian Information (Physical Activity, Nutrients, and Body Adaptations)

14-1 Monitoring Physical Activity in Canada

The Canadian Fitness and Lifestyle Research Institute monitors the physical activity of Canadians, providing data for each of the provinces and the territories, as a group (North)[1]. Data is collected and analyzed from the National Population Health Surveys and the Canadian Community Health Survey (CCHS). The estimate from the 2002/2003 CCHS is that 51% of Canadian adults are physically inactive (http://www.cflri.ca/eng/statistics/surveys/pam2004.php). The report indicates that the level of physical inactivity decreased between the late 1990s and 2002; more women than men are physically inactive; and physical inactivity increases with age. The latest goal set by the Federal, Provincial and Territorial (FPT) Ministers responsible for Physical Activity, Recreation and Sport in 2003 was to reduce physical inactivity by 10% by 2010 (http://www.phac-aspc.gc.ca/hl-vs-strat/) but in the fall of 2005 they also approved "The Integrated Pan-Canadian Healthy Living Strategy" which includes a new set of targets for increases in healthy eating, physical activity and healthy weights by 2015 (see below).

"The Integrated Pan-Canadian Healthy Living Strategy" 2005 targets are:

Healthy Eating
By 2015, increase by 20% the proportion of Canadians who make healthy food choices according to the Canadian Community Health Survey (CCHS), and Statistics Canada (SC)/Canadian Institute for Health Information (CIHI) health Indicators.

Physical Activity
By 2015, increase by 20% the proportion of Canadians who participate in regular physical activity based on 30 minutes/day of moderate to vigorous activity as measured by the CCHS and the Physical Activity Benchmarks/ Monitoring Program.

Healthy Weights
By 2015, increase by 20% the proportion of Canadians at a "normal" body weight based on a Body Mass Index (BMI) of 18.5 to 24.9 as measured by the National Population Health Survey (NPHS), CCHS, and SC/CIHI health indicators.

http://www.phac-aspc.gc.ca/hl-vs-strat/pdf/hls_e.pdf

14-2 Physical Activity Guides to Healthy Active Living

Health Canada publishes the *Physical Activity Guide to Healthy Active Living* to encourage Canadians to be more active. A summary statement from the guide is presented in **Appendix I-7, Figure I-1** in the textbook. Also, see Section 14-3 below for an excerpt from the guide. It is supported by the *Handbook for Physical Activity Guide to Healthy Active Living*, which can be ordered from the Physical Activity Guide web site. The guide supports the inclusion of physical activity information within a healthy lifestyle. Physical activity guides for seniors, children, youth and families with either children or youth are also available from the Physical Activity Guide web site (www.paguide.com).

14-3 *Canada's Physical Activity Guide to Healthy Active Living:*

Choose a variety of activities from these three groups

Endurance: 4 – 7 days a week
Continuous activities for your heart, lungs and circulatory system.

Flexibility: 4 -7 days a week
Gentle reaching bending and stretching activities to keep your muscles relaxed and joints mobile.

Strength: 2 – 4 days a week
Activities against resistance to strengthen muscles and bones and improve posture

14-4 Nutrition and Physical Activity on the Net – Canadian

- Coalition for Active Living – www.activeliving.ca

- Canadian Fitness and Lifestyle Research Institute - http://www.cflri.ca/ .

- Coaching Association of Canada – www.coach.ca

_____

References Cited

[1]. Canadian Fitness and Lifestyle Research 2003 Physical Activity Monitor
http://www.cflri.ca/eng/statistics/surveys/pam2003.php (accessed June 06, 2007).

Highlight 14 – Supplements as Ergogenic Aids

Should They Be Considered Breakthroughs, Gimmicks or Dangers?

In Canada, many of the ergogenic aids described in the **Highlight** for Chapter 14 (also see chapter **Glossary**) of the textbook are regulated under the Natural Health Products regulations. To find out about ergogenic products and claims that are permitted in Canada, check the Natural Health Products Directorate web site at www.hc-sc.gc.ca/hpfb-dgpsa/nhpd-dpsn/index_e.html. (accessed June 06, 2007)

Further readings on Ergogenic Aids:

- Williams MH. Nutrition for health fitness & sport (8th ed) 2007 McGraw-Hill, Toronto ON.

- Kreider RB, Leutholtz B. Optimizing nutrition for exercise and sport. In Temple NJ, Wilson T, Jacobs DR Jr (eds). Nutritional Health: Strategies for Disease Prevention, 2nd ed. Humana Press, New Jersey, 2006, p. 313-346.

- Wolinsky I, and Driskell JA. (editors). Nutritional Ergogenic Aids. 2004 CRC Press.   Boca Raton FL

- Bahrke MS, Yesalis CE. (editors) Performance Enhancing Substances in Sport and Exercise. 2002 Human Kinetics, Windsor ON

- Position of Dietitians of Canada, the American Dietetic Association and the American College of Sports Medicine: Nutrition and Athletic Performance Can J Diet Prac Res 2000; 61; 176-192.

Canadian Food Inspection Agency - Letter to Sports Nutrition Industry, June 2002. http://www.inspection.gc.ca/english/fssa/labeti/inform/20020624e.shtml (a follow up inspection of sports nutrition meal replacements and nutritional supplements that involved 52 inspections in 31 cities across Canada between September and October 2004, was conducted. Watch CFIA's website for the Official results http://www.inspection.gc.ca/english/toce.shtml).

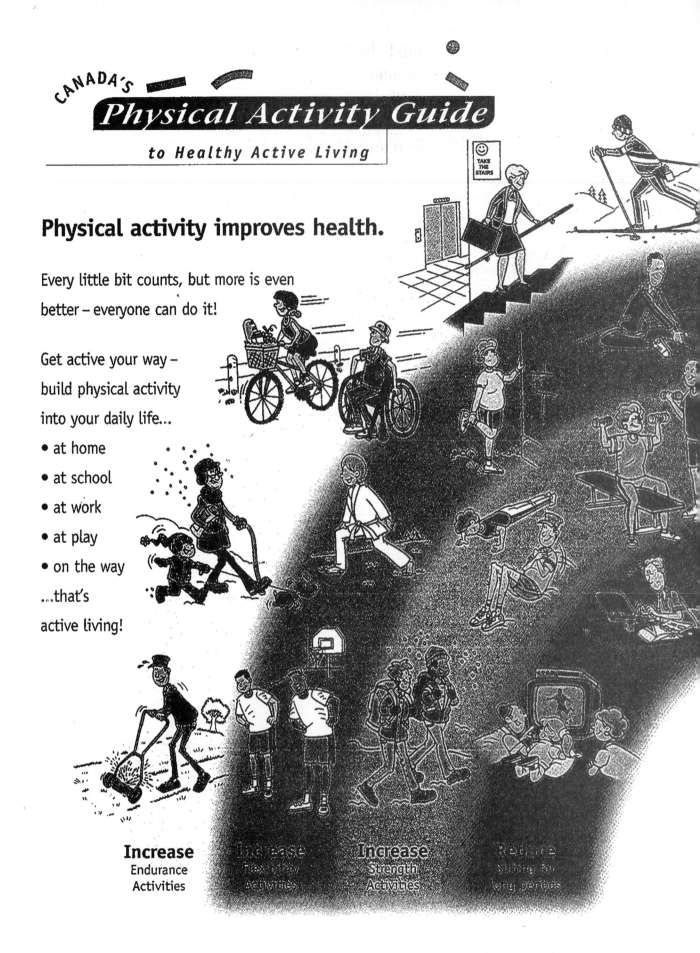

Canada's *Physical Activity Guide*

to Healthy Active Living

Physical activity improves health.

Every little bit counts, but more is even better – everyone can do it!

Get active your way – build physical activity into your daily life...

- at home
- at school
- at work
- at play
- on the way

...that's active living!

TAKE THE STAIRS

Increase
Endurance
Activities

Increase
Flexibility
Activities

Increase
Strength
Activities

Reduce
Sitting for
long periods

Health Canada   Santé Canada

CSEP SCPE   Canadian Society Exercise Physiology

Choose a variety of activities from these three groups:

Endurance

4-7 days a week
Continuous activities for your heart, lungs and circulatory system.

Flexibility

4-7 days a week
Gentle reaching, bending and stretching activities to keep your muscles relaxed and joints mobile.

Strength

2-4 days a week
Activities against resistance to strengthen muscles and bones and improve posture.

Starting slowly is very safe for most people. Not sure? Consult your health professional.

For a copy of the *Guide Handbook* and more information:
1-888-334-9769, or
www.paguide.com

Eating well is also important. Follow *Canada's Food Guide to Healthy Eating* to make wise food choices.

Get Active Your Way, Every Day – For Life!

Scientists say accumulate 60 minutes of physical activity every day to stay healthy or improve your health. As you progress to moderate activities you can cut down to 30 minutes, 4 days a week. Add-up your activities in periods of at least 10 minutes each. Start slowly..... and build up.

Time needed depends on effort

Very Light Effort	Light Effort *60 minutes*	Moderate Effort *30-60 minutes*	Vigorous Effort *20-30 minutes*	Maximum Effort
• Strolling	• Light walking	• Brisk walking	• Aerobics	• Sprinting
• Dusting	• Volleyball	• Biking	• Jogging	• Racing
	• Easy gardening	• Raking leaves	• Hockey	
	• Stretching	• Swimming	• Basketball	
		• Dancing	• Fast swimming	
		• Water aerobics	• Fast dancing	

Range needed to stay healthy

You Can Do It – Getting started is easier than you think

Physical activity doesn't have to be very hard. Build physical activities into your daily routine.

- Walk whenever you can – get off the bus early, use the stairs instead of the elevator.
- Reduce inactivity for long periods, like watching TV.
- Get up from the couch and stretch and bend for a few minutes every hour.
- Play actively with your kids.
- Choose to walk, wheel or cycle for short trips.

- Start with a 10 minute walk – gradually increase the time.
- Find out about walking and cycling paths nearby and use them.
- Observe a physical activity class to see if you want to try it.
- Try one class to start, you don't have to make a long-term commitment.
- Do the activities you are doing now, more often.

Benefits of regular activity:

- better health
- improved fitness
- better posture and balance
- better self-esteem
- weight control
- stronger muscles and bones
- feeling more energetic
- relaxation and reduced stress
- continued independent living in later life

Health risks of inactivity:

- premature death
- heart disease
- obesity
- high blood pressure
- adult-onset diabetes
- osteoporosis
- stroke
- depression
- colon cancer

Chapter 15 Canadian Information (Life Cycle Nutrition: Pregnancy and Lactation)

15-1 Canadian Statistics on Perinatal Health

The infant mortality rate in Canada tends to be lower than that in the United States 7/1000 live births), with the rate of 5.3 deaths per 1,000 in 2004, a decrease from 6.5 deaths per 1000 in 1995[1]. You can find perinatal statistics and other information about perinatal health behaviours by province from the Health Canada Perinatal Report 2003 (http://www.phac-aspc.gc.ca/publicat/cphr-rspc03/index.html). Information about infant and child health from the Canadian Paediatric Surveillance Program is available at http://www.phac-aspc.gc.ca/publicat/cpsp-pcsp03/page3_e.html.

15-2 Folic Acid and Pregnancy: The Canadian Situation

Folic acid fortification is also having an impact on the folic acid status of Canadian pregnant women. Information about the folic acid issue in Canada can be found at http://www.hc-sc.gc.ca/iyh-vsv/med/folic-folique_e.html.

If you are interested in folate nutrition and pregnancy in Canada you will find the following journal articles and promotional materials useful.

O'Connor D.L. Four years after enhanced folic acid fortification of the Canadian food supply – How are we doing? *Canadian Journal of Public Health* 93(2002):245-246.

Ray J. G., M.J.Vermeulen, S.C. Boss, D.E.C. Cole. Declining rate of folate insufficiency among adults following increased folic acid food fortification in Canada. *Canadian Journal of Public Health* 93(2002):249-253.

Reisch H.S., M.A.T. Flynn. Folic acid and the prevention of neural tube defects (NTDs): Challenges and recommendations for public health. *Canadian Journal of Public Health* 93(2002):254-258.

Gucciardi E, Pietrusiak MA, Reynolds DL, Pouleau J. 2002. Incidence of neural tube defects in Ontario, 1986-1999. CMAJ 167 (3): 237-240.

Liu S, West R, Randell E, Longerich L, Steel O'Connor K, Scott H, Crowley M, Lam A, Prabhakaran V and McCourt C, A comprehensive evaluation of food fortification with folic acid for the primary prevention of neural tube defects. *BMC Pregnancy and childbirth 2004; 4: 20 (1-10).*

Health Canada has a campaign to increase awareness of the need for folic acid. Promotional materials can be found at http://www.phac-aspc.gc.ca/fa-af/index.html .

15-3 Canadian Prenatal Guidelines

The Canadian recommendations for preconceptional and prenatal nutrition care are found in Nutrition for a Healthy Pregnancy: National Guidelines for the Childbearing Years, published by Health Canada[2]. The guidelines have been endorsed by Dietitians of Canada, The Society of Obstetricians and Gynaecologists of Canada, and members of the Federal/Provincial/Territorial Group on Nutrition. The guidelines recommend gestational weight gain, based on pre-pregnancy body mass index similar to the recommendations in **Table 15.1** of the textbook. These recommendations are in Table 15-1 of this section.

The national guidelines also discuss problem nutrients, suggested food patterns, and recommendations for problems such as gestational diabetes mellitus, pre-eclampsia, morning sickness, and constipation. The full guidelines document can provide you with an appreciation of the Canadian food and nutrition issues and recommendations for pregnancy.

Table 15-1 Canadian Recommendations for Gestational Weight Gain[a]

BMI Category (Pre-Pregnancy)	Recommended Total Gestational Gain	
	kg	lb.
<20	12.5 - 18.0	28 - 40
20 - 25	11.5 - 16.0	25 - 35
>27	7.0 - 11.5	15 - 25

[a] Health Canada. *Nutrition for a Healthy Pregnancy: National Guidelines for the Childbearing Years.* Ottawa: Minister of Public Works and Government Services, 1999. http://www.hc-sc.gc.ca/fn-an/nutrition/prenatal/national_guidelines-lignes_directrices_nationales-06e_e.html

15-4 Fetal Alcohol Syndrome

In 1996, Health Canada and the Canadian Paediatric Society released a joint statement on Fetal Alcohol Syndrome and Fetal Alcohol Effects[3]. The basis of the recommendations is that "the prudent choice for women who are or may become pregnant is to abstain from alcohol." It also recommends that health professionals inform pregnant women who have consumed small amounts of alcohol occasionally that the risk is minimal. They should also tell them that both mother and fetus will benefit if the mother stops drinking alcohol at any time during the pregnancy. This statement is available through the Health Canada Nutrition web site (http://www.hc-sc.gc.ca/ahc-asc/pubs/drugs-drogues/symposium_alcohol-alcool/christine_e.html) and is consistent with the 1999 Nutrition for a Healthy Pregnancy: National Guidelines for the Childbearing Years[2]. Client education related to preventing fetal alcohol syndrome is part of the Canadian Prenatal Nutrition Program.

In December 2003, the Public Health Agency of Canada announced 'Fetal Alcohol Spectrum Disorder (FASD): A Framework for Action' in an effort to help frontline health workers prevent it and improve outcomes for those with FASD (approximately 9 in every 1000 are born with FASD). See http://www.phac-aspc.gc.ca/dca-dea/publications/fasd-etcaf/index.html (accessed July 07, 2006). Education materials include a booklet and a 2006 article on FASD see (http://www.phac-aspc.gc.ca/fasd-etcaf/publications_e.html). These, and other materials, can be also be accessed through the Public Health Agency of Canada's web site for the Division of Childhood and Adolescence http://www.phac-aspc.gc.ca/dca-dea/7-18yrs-ans/hbschealth_e.html .

15-5 Canadian Prenatal Programs

Although Canada does not have a single national nutrition program for pregnant women, supportive nutrition programs are available to them. The Canada Prenatal Nutrition Program (CPNP) first announced by Health Canada in 1994 is now available from the Public Health Agency of Canada's website for the Division of Childhood and Adolescence. The CPNP provides food supplementation, nutrition counselling, support, education, referral, and counselling on lifestyle issues for women who are most likely to have unhealthy babies[4]. The program also supports community-based services by funding local community groups to establish and deliver services according to the local population needs and build on existing prenatal programs. The women targeted by this program include pregnant adolescents, youth at risk of becoming pregnant, pregnant women who abuse alcohol or other substances, pregnant women living in violent situations, off-reserve aboriginals and Inuit, refugees, and pregnant women living in isolation or not having access to services. The CPNP is jointly managed by the federal government and provincial/territorial governments. In 2002, there were 350 CPNP projects funded by the Public and Population Health Branch (PPHB) serving over 2,000 communities across Canada[4]. In addition, over 550 CPNP projects were funded by the First Nations and Inuit Health Branch in Inuit and on-reserve First Nation communities. You can get the most current information about the Canadian Prenatal Nutrition Program from the web site, www.phac-aspc.gc.ca/dca-dea/programs-mes/cpnp_main_e.html, or check with your local public health department to find the Canada Prenatal Nutrition Program in your community.

Many public health departments or community health agencies offer prenatal and postnatal education programs to interested members of the community. To find out about programs for pregnant women at nutritional risk in your locality, see http://cpnp-pcnp.phac-aspc.gc.ca/ or contact your local or provincial public health department.

15-6 Canadian Recommendations for Lactation

Breastfeeding is discussed on pages 45 to 50 in Nutrition for a Healthy Pregnancy: National Guidelines for the Childbearing Years[2]. Eating Well with Canada's Food Guide recommends that women who breastfeed "Include an extra 2 to 3 Food Guide Servings each day" http://www.hc-sc.gc.ca/fn-an/alt_formats/hpfb-dgpsa/pdf/food-guide-aliment/print_eatwell_bienmang_e.pdf . However, concern has been raised about the nutritional adequacy of the food intake of women who are breastfeeding, e.g., one of the few studies about food intake by lactating women in low-income communities is provided by Doran and Evers[5].

15-7 Nutrition for Healthy Term Infants

The current guidelines for infant feeding "Nutrition for Healthy Term Infants"[6] were prepared and approved by the Canadian Paediatric Society, Dietitians of Canada and Health Canada. The document provides an excellent overview of issues involved with infant feeding. The complete document (including important recent updates about Vit D) can be found through Health Canada's up-dated web site for Nutrition for Healthy Term Infants (http://www.hc-sc.gc.ca/fn-an/pubs/infant-nourrisson/nut_infant_nourrisson_term_e.html#table).

However, in 2004, Health Canada announced their latest recommendation for exclusive breastfeeding, which is now "… for the first six months of life for healthy term infants"[7]. This recommendation also includes introducing "nutrient-rich solid foods with particular attention to iron at six months with continued breastfeeding for up to two years and beyond." Fact sheets that would be suitable for student reading are available at http://www.hc-sc.gc.ca/fn-an/nutrition/child-enfant/infant-nourisson/breastfed-nourrissons-rec_e.html. Thus, new detailed guidelines for feeding healthy term infants in Canada must soon be developed.

Many public health professionals are concerned about the promotion of infant formulas in Canada and its effect on breastfeeding rate and duration. The Infant Feeding Action Coalition (INFACT, www.infactcanada.ca) Canada is among the non-governmental, non-profit organizations that work to improve the health and well-being of infants and young children through the protection, promotion and support of breastfeeding. The most recent information about breastfeeding rates and educational materials on breastfeeding can be found by completing a search on the Health Canada web site for "Breastfeeding." Much of the information is found through the web site for the Public Health Agency of Canada's website for Health Promotion at (http://www.phac-aspc.gc.ca/dca-dea/prenatal/nutrition e.html).

In 2004, Health Canada updated the recommendation for vitamin D supplementation, recommending that all breastfed, healthy term infants in Canada receive a daily vitamin D supplement of 10 μg (400 IU)[8]. The statement goes on to recommend that "supplementation should begin at birth and continue until the infant's diet includes at least 10 μg (400 IU) per day of vitamin D from other dietary sources or until the breastfed infant reaches one year of age."

15-8 Infant Formulas in Canada

The nutrient composition of infant formulas in Canada is regulated by the Food and Drugs Act and Regulations[9] and varies slightly from those in the United States. Both Canadian and United States consumers who live close to the border may buy infant formula in the nearby country. Health professionals should advise parents who are buying infant formulas in the other country to look at the labels carefully, especially for iron content, which may be labelled differently. Recently, Canada joined numerous other countries who have infant formulae that are fortified with the omega-6 and omega-3 fatty acids, arachidonic acid and docosahexaenoic acid, respectively, fatty acids that support normal growth and development in healthy term and pre-term infants. See http://www.hc-sc.gc.ca/fn-an/gmf-agm/appro/dhasco arasco e.html (accessed June 07, 2007).

15-9 Iron Status of Canadian Infants

Iron status of infants continues to be a concern, especially in low income communities and First Nations and Inuit populations[10]. In some cases, there may be a link between anemia in the mother during pregnancy and the iron status of the infant[11].

15-10 Assessing and Monitoring Growth in Infants and Children

A recent collaborative statement on this issue from Dietitians of Canada, Canadian Paediatric Society, The College of Family Physicians of Canada and Community Health Nurses Association of Canada[12] outlines some of the tools available to health care professionals, such as CDC's gender specific / age appropriate growth charts "The Use of Growth Charts for Assessing and Monitoring Growth in Canadian Infants and Children".

References Cited

[1]. Statistics Canada: Health Status Indicators – Infant mortality rates by province and territory. http://www40.statcan.ca/l01/cst01/health21a.htm (accessed May 17, 2007)

2. Health Canada. *Nutrition for a Healthy Pregnancy: National Guidelines for the Childbearing Years*. Ottawa: Minister of Public Works and Government Services, 1999. http://www.hc-sc.gc.ca/fn-an/nutrition/prenatal/national_guidelines-lignes_directrices_nationales-06e_e.html (accessed June 07, 2007).

3. Health Canada and The Canadian Paediatric Society. *Joint Statement on Fetal Alcohol Syndrome and Fetal Alcohol Effects*. Ottawa, 1996.

4. Public Health Agency of Canada. *Canada Prenatal Nutrition Program*. http://www.phac-aspc.gc.ca/dca-dea/programs-mes/cpnp_main_e.html, (accessed July 07, 2006).

5. Doran L and S Evers. Energy and nutrient inadequacies in the diets of low-income women who breast-feed. *J Am. Diet Assoc*. 97(1997):1283-1287.

6. Nutrition for healthy term infants. Statement of the joint working Group: Canadian Pediatric Society, Dietitians of Canada and Health Canada, Ministry of Public Works and Government Services, Ottawa. [For a summary of the contents of this document see *Nutrition for healthy term infants. Canadian Journal of Diet Practice and Research* (formerly J Can Diet Assoc) 59(1998):93-96].

7. Exclusive Breastfeeding Duration - 2004 Health Canada Recommendation http://www.hc-sc.gc.ca/fn-an/nutrition/child-enfant/infant-nourisson/excl_bf_dur-dur_am_excl_e.html (accessed July 07, 2006).

8. Health Canada. Vitamin D Supplementation for Breastfed Infants – 2004 Health Canada Recommendation. http://www.hc-sc.gc.ca/fn-an/nutrition/child-enfant/infant-nourisson/vita_d_supp_e.html (accessed July 07, 2006).

9. Health and Welfare Canada. *Departmental Consolidation of the Food and Drugs Act and Regulations*. Ottawa: Ministry of Supply and Services, 2004. http://www.hc-sc.gc.ca/fn-an/legislation/acts-lois/fda-lad/index_e.html (accessed July 07, 2006).

10. N.D. Wollows, E. Dewailly, K. Gray-Donald, Anemia and iron status in Inuit infants from Northern Quebec. *Canadian Journal of Public Health* 91(2000):407-410.

11. N. Savoie, F.M. Rioux. Impact of maternal anemia on the infant's iron status at 9 months of age. *Canadian Journal of Public Health* 93 (2002):203-207.

12. The Use of Growth Charts for Assessing and Monitoring Growth in Canadian Infants and Children. A collaborative statement from Dietitians of Canada, Canadian Paediatric Society, The College of Family Physicians of Canada and Community Health Nurses Association of Canada. *Can J Diet Pract Res; March 2004 65: 22-32*. http://www.cps.ca/english/statements/N/cps04-01.htm (accessed June 07, 2007).

HIGHLIGHT 15: Fetal Alcohol Syndrome

See **Sections 15-2** and **15-4** above.

Chapter 16 Canadian Information (Life Cycle Nutrition: Infancy, Childhood and Adolescence)

INFANCY:

16-1 Nutrition for Healthy Term Infants

The current guidelines for infant feeding "Nutrition for Healthy Term Infants"[1] were prepared and approved by the Canadian Paediatric Society, Dietitians of Canada and Health Canada. The document provides an excellent overview of issues involved with infant feeding. The complete document (including important recent updates about Vit D) can be found through Health Canada's up-dated web site for Nutrition for Healthy Term Infants (http://www.hc-sc.gc.ca/fn-an/pubs/infant-nourrisson/nut_infant_nourrisson_term_e.html#table).

However, in 2004, Health Canada announced their latest recommendation for exclusive breastfeeding, which is now "… for the first six months of life for healthy term infants"[2]. This recommendation also includes introducing "nutrient-rich solid foods with particular attention to iron at six months with continued breastfeeding for up to two years and beyond." Fact sheets that would be suitable for student reading are available at http://www.hc-sc.gc.ca/fn-an/nutrition/child-enfant/infant-nourisson/breastfed-nourrissons-rec_e.html. Thus, new detailed guidelines for feeding healthy term infants in Canada must soon be developed.

Many public health professionals are concerned about the promotion of infant formulas in Canada and its effect on breastfeeding rate and duration. The Infant Feeding Action Coalition (INFACT, www.infactcanada.ca) Canada is among the non-governmental, non-profit organizations that work to improve the health and well-being of infants and young children through the protection, promotion and support of breastfeeding. The most recent information about breastfeeding rates and educational materials on breastfeeding can be found by completing a search on the Health Canada web site for "Breastfeeding." Much of the information is found through the web site for the Public Health Agency of Canada's website for Health Promotion at (http://www.phac-aspc.gc.ca/dca-dea/prenatal/nutrition_e.html).

In 2004, Health Canada updated the recommendation for vitamin D supplementation, recommending that all breastfed, healthy term infants in Canada receive a daily vitamin D supplement of 10 µg (400 IU)[3]. The statement goes on to recommend that "supplementation should begin at birth and continue until the infant's diet includes at least 10 µg (400 IU) per day of vitamin D from other dietary sources or until the breastfed infant reaches one year of age."

16-2 Infant Formulas in Canada

The nutrient composition of infant formulas in Canada is regulated by the Food and Drugs Act and Regulations[4] and varies slightly from those in the United States. Both Canadian and United States consumers who live close to the border may buy infant formula in the nearby country. Health professionals should advise parents who are buying infant formulas in the other country to look at the labels carefully, especially for iron content, which may be labelled differently. Recently, Canada joined numerous other countries who have infant formulae that are fortified with the omega-6 and omega-3 fatty acids, arachidonic acid and docosahexaenoic acid, respectively, fatty acids that support normal growth and development in healthy term and pre-term infants. See http://www.hc-sc.gc.ca/fn-an/gmf-agm/appro/dhasco_arasco_e.html (accessed July 07, 2006).

16-3 Iron Status of Canadian Infants

Iron status of infants continues to be a concern, especially in low income communities and First Nations and Inuit populations[5]. In some cases, there may be a link between anemia in the mother during pregnancy and the iron status of the infant[6].

16-4 Assessing and Monitoring Growth in Infants and Children

A recent collaborative statement on this issue from Dietitians of Canada, Canadian Paediatric Society, The College of Family Physicians of Canada and Community Health Nurses Association of Canada[7] outlines some of the tools available to health care professionals, such as CDC's gender specific / age appropriate growth charts "The Use of Growth Charts for Assessing and Monitoring Growth in Canadian Infants and Children".

References Cited

[1]. Nutrition for healthy term infants. Statement of the joint working Group: Canadian Pediatric Society, Dietitians of Canada and Health Canada, Ministry of Public Works and Government Services, Ottawa. [For a summary of the contents of this document see *Nutrition for healthy term infants. Canadian Journal of Diet Practice and Research* (formerly J Can Diet Assoc) 59(1998):93-96].

[2]. Exclusive Breastfeeding Duration - 2004 Health Canada Recommendation http://www.hc-sc.gc.ca/fn-an/nutrition/child-enfant/infant-nourisson/excl_bf_dur-dur_am_excl_e.html (accessed July 07, 2006).

[3]. Health Canada. Vitamin D Supplementation for Breastfed Infants – 2004 Health Canada Recommendation. http://www.hc-sc.gc.ca/fn-an/nutrition/child-enfant/infant-nourisson/vita_d_supp_e.html (accessed July 07, 2006).

[4]. Health and Welfare Canada. *Departmental Consolidation of the Food and Drugs Act and Regulations.* Ottawa: Ministry of Supply and Services, 2004. http://www.hc-sc.gc.ca/fn-an/legislation/acts-lois/fda-lad/index_e.html (accessed July 07, 2006).

[5]. N.D. Wollows, E. Dewailly, K. Gray-Donald, Anemia and iron status in Inuit infants from Northern Quebec. *Canadian Journal of Public Health* 91(2000):407-410.

[6]. N. Savoie, F.M. Rioux. Impact of maternal anemia on the infant's iron status at 9 months of age. *Canadian Journal of Public Health* 93 (2002):203-207.

[7] The Use of Growth Charts for Assessing and Monitoring Growth in Canadian Infants and Children. A collaborative statement from Dietitians of Canada, Canadian Paediatric Society, The College of Family Physicians of Canada and Community Health Nurses Association of Canada. *Paediatrics & Child Health* 2004;9(3):171-180 http://www.cps.ca/english/statements/N/cps04-01.htm (accessed June 07, 2007).

CHILDHOOD AND ADOLESCENCE:

16-5 Eating Well with Canada's Food Guide – Children 2-3 Years Old.

Note: the recommendation for Milk and Alternatives is 2 Food Guide Servings per day and the directional statement "Have 500 mL (2 cups) of milk every day for adequate vitamin D" see **Figure 16-1** below.

Figure 16-1 Recommended Number of Food Guide Servings for Children 2-3 Years of Age[‡]

Food Group	Number of Food Guide Servings	Examples of One Child-size Serving
Vegetables and Fruit	4 "Have vegetables and fruit more often than juice"	- 1 medium-size vegetable or fruit - 125 mL (¼-½ cup) fresh, frozen or canned vegetables or fruit - 250 mL (1 cup) leafy vegetables - 125 mL (½ cup) juice
Grain Products	3 "Make at least half your grain products whole grain each day"	- 1 slice of bread - 30 g cold cereal - 125 mL (½ cup) hot cereal - ½ bagel, pita or bun - 125 mL (½ cup) cooked pasta or rice
Milk and Alternatives	2 "Have 500 mL (2 cups) of milk every day for adequate vitamin D"	- 250 mL (I cup) milk or fortified soy beverage - 50 g cheese - 175 mL (¾ cup) yogurt
Meat and Alternatives	1 "Have meat alternatives such as beans, lentils and tofu often"	75 g meat, fish or poultry 175 mL (¾ cup) cooked legumes 175 mL (¾ cup) tofu 30 mL (2 Tbsp) peanut butter

[‡] Adapted from Health Canada. Eating Well with Canada's Food Guide. Ottawa: Minister of Health 2007. Cat: H164-38/1-2007E.

16-6 Health Behaviours of Canadian Children / Adolescents

Eating and other health behaviours of Canadian children were reported in Health Behaviour in School-Aged Children, part of an international longitudinal study from 1983 to 1998. This report can be found through the web site for the Public Health Agency of Canada at www.phac-aspc.gc.ca/dca-dea/7-18yrs-ans/hbschealth_e.html and provides data on specific behaviours for different age groups between 7 and 18 years of age. The next survey is planned for 2005/2006.

The food sources of nutrients for **adolescents** in the national study on Food Habits of Canadians also provides information about adolescent food intake[1].

Examples of national healthy living strategies targeted toward school-aged children include the government's 'Integrated Pan-Canadian Healthy Living Strategy' (http://www.phac-aspc.gc.ca/hl-vs-strat/ppt/synopsis.html) and the LONG LIVE KIDS campaign, a one-of-a-kind Canadian collaboration between industry, issue experts and the government that provides tools for a balanced lifestyle (healthy eating, active living, media literacy). You may have seen TV spots promoting this latter campaign where a blue character on a T-shirt shows us how to 'balance food and activity', otherwise you might turn to "goo" (http://www.longlivekids.ca/llk.html).

16-7 School Food Policy

Canada is the only developed country in the world that has no national policy or program for feeding school children. Some provinces or local boards of education, often in collaboration with pubic health departments, are developing school food policies to address availability and quality of food in schools and the nutrition curriculum[2]. Teacher associations are showing great concern for the hungry children in classrooms and many schools have developed some type of feeding program. If interested, check with your local board of education to get details on local programs and policies for foods in schools. In Canada, a Resolution by the Alberta Public Health Association[3] and the Ontario Ministry of Education[4] have issued guidelines for food and beverages that can be sold in vending machines in elementary schools in hopes of reducing childhood obesity. Details on the latter guidelines can be found at www.edu.gov.on.ca/eng/document/reports/healthyschools/index.html. The Ontario guidelines were based largely on reports from the Ontario Society of Nutrition Professionals in Public Health (OSNPPH) Nutrition Workgroup Steering Committee and Dietitians of Canada.

School feeding programs are often looking for student volunteers. The Canadian Living Foundation: Breakfast for Learning provides resources for breakfast programs for children (http://www.breakfastforlearning.ca/english/index.html). This non-profit organization is helping out in over 6,900 communities in every province and territory in Canada. You might also have heard that Shania Twain, an internationally recognized Canadian singer, promotes and fundraises for this national organization that is solely dedicated to supporting child nutrition.

References Cited

[1]. S. Phillips, L.J. Starkey, K. Gray-Donald. Food habits of Canadians: Food sources of nutrients for the adolescent sample. *Canadian Journal of Dietetic Practice and Research* 65(2004):81-84.

[2]. M.L. McKenna. Issues in implementing school nutrition policies. *Canadian Journal of Dietetic Practice and Research* 64(2003):208-213.

[3] Elimination of Soft Drink Promotion in Schools, Resolution 6, Alberta Public Health Association (2003).

[4] Minister of Education. Making Ontario Schools Healthier Places to Learn. Ontario Ministry of Education, October 2004.

Highlight 16: Childhood Obesity and Early Development of Chronic Diseases

H16.1 Childhood Obesity in Canada

Studies show that Canadian children, aged 7 to 13 years, are becoming progressively overweight and obese[1]. From 1981 to 1996, BMI (based on self- / proxy-reported data) increased at a rate of nearly 0.1 kg/m^2 per year for both sexes at most ages. Prevalence of overweight (>85th age- and sex-specific percentile increased in boys from 15% in 1981 to 28.8% in 1996; in girls from 15% to 23.6%. During the same period, prevalence of obesity (>95th age- and sex-specific percentile) increased from 5% to 13.5% for boys and 5% to 11.8% for girls.

Overweight among children is an important health issue in Canada. Although there are limited data on childhood obesity in Canada, some information is available. For example, information about factors that influence eating and activity among children in Nova Scotia communities has been published by the Canadian Diabetes Association[2]. An article on the Effectiveness of School Programs in Preventing Childhood Obesity[3] and information on breakfast consumption, smoking and physical activity have also been reported for some Ontario adolescents[4]. Many Canadian health researchers also feel that directly measured height and weight data for children are essential in order to obtain a valid picture of childhood overweight / obesity in Canada[5].

More recent data from the Canadian Community Health Survey (2004) Cycle 2.2 using measured data revealed that for children 2-17 yrs, 18% were considered overweight and 8% were considered obese, a combined rate of 26% (http://www.statcan.ca/english/research/82-620-MIE/2005001/pdf/cobesity.pdf) .

Further information on other aspects of the health of Canadian children and adolescents can be found at the web site for the Public Health Agency of Canada's Division of Childhood and Adolescence, http://www.phac-aspc.gc.ca/dca-dea/main_e.html.

References Cited

[1]. M.R. Tremblay, J.D. Willms. Secular trends in the body mass index of Canadian children. *Canadian Medical Association Journal* 163 (2000): 1429-33.

[2]. Canadian Diabetes Association. Barriers and Enablers to Healthy Eating and Active Living in Children: Key Findings in 6 Nova Scotia Communities. Toronto, 2002.

[3]. Veugelers PJ and Fitzgerald AL, MSc. Effectiveness of School Programs in Preventing Childhood Obesity: A Multilevel Comparison. *Amer Journal of Public Health March 2005; 95(3): 432-435.*

[4]. B. Cohen, S. Evers, S. Manske, K. Cercovitz, H.G. Edward. Smoking, physical activity and breakfast consumption among secondary school students in a southwestern Ontario community. *Canadian Journal of Public Health* 94(2003):41-44.

[5] Tremblay M. The Need for Directly Measured Health Data in Canada. *Canadian Journal of Public Health* 2004; 95: 165-166.

Chapter 17 Canadian Information (Life Cycle Nutrition: Adulthood and the Later Years)

17-1 Nutrition and Women's Health

A recently released Position statement on Nutrition and Women's Health by ADA and DC outlines some of women's specific nutritional needs and unique risk factors for nutrition-related chronic diseases[1]. Also see other resources, such as, the Dietitians of Canada factsheet "Women take on Healthy Eating". It outlines key nutrition challenges for women and specifies recommendations and food sources for important nutrients like calcium, iron and fiber (http://www.dietitians.ca/public/content/eat_well_live_well/english/faqs_tips_facts/fact_sheets/index.asp?fn=view&id=1331&idstring=1331).

17-2 Canadian Programs for Seniors

Although there are no Canadian national programs focused on nutrition for the elderly population, many provinces and municipalities offer meals-on-wheels and congregate dining programs, as well as other activities and services to support the aging population. Information about healthy aging and nutrition can be found through the Government of Canada's Bulletin "Expression" of the National Advisory Council on Aging. For example, see 'Eat well to Age well' Vol 17 (3) 2004 (go to August 2004 at http://www.phac-aspc.gc.ca/seniors-aines/archive/archive2004_e.htm) as well as links to a host of publications on aging and health on the Public Health Agency of Canada's Division of Aging and Seniors web site (http://www.phac-aspc.gc.ca/seniors-aines/index_pages/publications_e.htm).

One example of a community-based nutrition education program is Evergreen Action Nutrition, provided by the Guelph/Wellington Seniors Association at the Evergreen Seniors Centre[2]. This program includes cooking workshops, men's cooking groups, monthly displays with recipes and pamphlets and individual counselling by a registered dietitian that are based on suggestions from community seniors. If interested, check in your community for nutrition programs for seniors.

Other healthy lifestyle resources for seniors include the Physical Activity Guide to Healthy Active Living for Older Adults. Both a tear sheet and a handbook are available from local health units and or the Public Health Agency of Canada's Physical Activity Unit web site: www.phac-aspc.gc.ca/pau-uap/paguide/older/index.html.

17-3 Nutrition Screening Tool for Canadian Seniors

Seniors in the Community: Risk Evaluation for Eating and Nutrition (SCREEN) was developed[3] and validated[4] among seniors of varying health status, living in a community in southern Ontario. Although similar to the one outlined in **Table 17.5** of the textbook (DETERMINE, Risk Factors for Malnutrition in Older Adults), this screening tool is used to identify seniors at risk for nutrition problems and to plan programs and services to address them. The screening tool was the basis for the Canadian-wide project, Bringing Nutrition Screening to Seniors. Information about this program can be found at the Dietitians of Canada web site, www.dietitians.ca/seniors/index.asp . This web site also provides access to other resources for seniors.

17-4 Canadian Readings and Resources

- H.H. Keller, H. Haresign, B Brockest. Process Evaluation of Bringing Nutrition Screening to Seniors in Canada (BNSS). *Canadian Journal of Dietetic Practice and Research* 68(2007):86-91.

- B. Shatenstein, S. Nadon, G. Ferland. Diet quality among older Quebecers as assessed by simple indicators. *Canadian Journal of Dietetic Practice and Research* 64(2003): 174-180.

- H.H. Keller, J.D. McKenzie. Nutritional risk in vulnerable community-living seniors. *Canadian Journal of Dietetic Practice and Research* 64(2003): 195-201.

- Garcia AC, Johnson CS. Development of educational modules for the promotion of healthy eating and physical activity among immigrant older adults. *Journal of Nutrition for the Elderly* 2003; 22 (3): 79-96.

- Johnson CS, Garcia AC. Dietary and activity profiles of selected immigrant older adults in Canada. *Journal of Nutrition for the Elderly*, 2003; 23 (1): 23-39.

- Canadian Centre for Activity and Aging (CCAA) – http://www.uwo.ca/actage/

- Canadian Association of Gerontology - http://www.cagacg.ca/whoweare/200_e.php

- Public Health Agency of Canada: Aging and Seniors - http://www.phac-aspc.gc.ca/seniors-aines/index_pages/publications_e.htm

- The Arthritis Society - www.arthritis.ca

- Nutrition Resource Centre – www.nutritionrc.ca

References

[1] Nutrition and Women's Health: Position of the American Dietetic Association and Dietitians of Canada. *Canadian Journal of Dietetic Practice and Research* 2004; 65:85-89

[2] M.R. Hedley, H.H. Keller, P.D. Vanderkooy, S.I. Kirkpatrick. Evergreen Action Nutrition: Lessons learned planning and implementing nutrition education for seniors using a community organization approach. *Journal of Nutrition for the Elderly* 21 (2002): 61-73.

[3] H.H. Keller, M.R. Hedley, S. Wong Brownlee. The development of Seniors in the Community: Risk Evaluation for Eating and Nutrition (SCREEN) *Canadian Journal of Dietetic Practice and Research* 61(2000):67-72.

[4] . H.H. Keller, J.D. McKenzie, R.E. Goy. Construct validation and test-retest reliability of the Seniors in the Community: Risk Evaluation for Eating and Nutrition Questionnaire. *Journal of Gerontology: MEDICAL SCIENCES* 56A(2001): M552-M558.

Highlight 17: Nutrient-Drug Interactions

Almost ten years ago, Health Canada was advising Canadians about Nutrient-Drug interactions, for example, the affect of grapefruit / grapefruit juice on certain calcium-channel blockers that may be prescribed for the treatment of high blood pressure, under certain circumstances (see http://www.hc-sc.gc.ca/dhp-mps/medeff/bulletin/carn-bcei_v7n4_e.html). Also, other foods (e.g., broccoli, liver) contain high levels of Vitamin K and Health Canada advises that such foods may alter the effects of warfarin, a blood thinner http://www.hc-sc.gc.ca/iyh-vsv/med/warfarin_e.html . Other examples of such interactions can be found in **Table H17.1** of the textbook. Thus, it is important that anyone concerned about this issue should check with their healthcare provider.

LECTURE OUTLINES: CHAPTER ONE

Chapter 18 Canadian Information (Diet and Health)

18-1 Leading Causes of Death in Canada

The leading causes of death in Canada tend to vary a little from those in the United States. The leading causes of death in Canada in 2001 are illustrated in Table 18-1 of this CSI Document. Note that, together, heart disease and stroke accounted for 34 % of deaths[1]. Canadian students should look for the most recent statistics for nutrition-related causes of mortality through the Statistics Canada web site (www.statscan.ca).

Table 18-1 Leading Causes of Death in Canada (2001)*

Heart Disease and Stroke	74,824 (34%)
Cancer	63,774 (29%)
Respiratory Disease	22,026 (10%)
Accidents, Suicides, Violence	13,996 (6%)
All other causes	41,797 (19%)

* Modified from from Statistics Canada: Major Causes of Death – Diseases of the circulatory system http://www43.statcan.ca/02/02b/02b_003_e.htm   (accessed June 25, 2007)

18-2 Canadian Recommendations for Dyslipidemia

A Canadian 'Working Group on Hypercholesterolemia and Other Lipemias' published their recommendations in 2003 for the management of dyslipidemia and prevention of cardiovascular disease[2] which use the same method for assessing ten-year risk of cardiovascular disease as explained in the exercise, "How to Assess Your Risk of Heart Disease," in the **"How To"** text box on page 631 of the textbook. The difference is that cholesterol levels in the Canadian version are expressed in mmol/L, instead of mg/dL as used in the textbook. The values in mmol/L are listed in Table 18-2 of this CSI Document.

Note: the latest "Diet and Lifestyle Recommendations Revision 2006 – A scientific Statement from the American Heart Association Nutrition Committee" was published in *Circulation* . 2006; 114: 82-96 or can be accessed on the American Heart Association website at http://www.americanheart.org/presenter.jhtml?identifier=851

Table 18-2 Cholesterol Values for Assessing 10 year Risk of Cardiovascular Disease in Canada
(adapted from McPherson t et al 2006 [2])

Total Cholesterol Level (mmol/L)

Total Cholesterol (mmol/L)	Risk Factors									
	Age 20-39 years		Age 40-49 years		Age 50-59 years		Age 60-69 years		Age 70-79 years	
	Men	Women	Men	Women	Men	Women	Men	Women	Men	Women
<4.14	0	0	0	0	0	0	0	0	0	0
4.15-5.19	4	4	3	3	2	2	1	1	0	1
5.20-6.19	7	8	5	6	3	4	1	2	0	1
6.20-7.20	9	11	6	8	4	5	2	3	1	2
≥7.21	11	13	8	10	5	7	3	4	1	2

HDL Cholesterol Level (mmol/L)

HDL-C (mmol/L)	Risk Factors	
	Men	Women
≥1.55	-1	-1
1.30-1.54	0	0
1.04-1.29	1	1
<1.04	2	2

18-3 Canadian Recommendations for Hypertension

The Canadian Hypertension Education Program (CHEP) released its latest Canadian guidelines on hypertension in January 2007[3.] They include a recommendation that the diagnosis should be expedited (i.e., using a strategy for diagnosis in fewer than "the up to 6 office visits over 6 months" as suggested in last year's recommendations). Thus, depending on a patient's global cardiovascular risk and recognizing factors other than hypertension, target values would be < 140 SBP/ 90 DBP mmHg or lower.

18-4 Canadian Resources for Diabetes

See Section 2-4 Diabetes Meal Planning Guide in Chapter 2 of this CSI Document and remember that the 'Good Health Eating Guide' has been revised and there is now (June 2006) a full 150 page manual entitled "Beyond the Basics: Meal Planning for Diabetes Prevention and Management". Check the Canadian Diabetes Association (CDA) web site for the most current information about this meal planning system (http://www.diabetes.ca/section_about/btb2006.asp) and how to order it. Note that information about Diabetes in languages other than English and French (e.g., Chinese) are available on CDA's website.

Prevention of diabetes is a priority of Health Canada, which introduced the Canadian Diabetes Strategy in 1999. This strategy has four components: 1) National Coordination, 2) Aboriginal Diabetes Initiative, 3) The National Diabetes Surveillance System, and 4) Prevention and Promotion. Current information about the programs and resources are available from the Health Canada web site: http://www.phac-aspc.gc.ca/ccdpc-cpcmc/diabetes-diabete/english/strategy/pp.html . The Canadian Diabetes Association has resources for the prevention and treatment of diabetes, including the 1) latest "2003 Clinical Practice Guidelines for the Prevention and Management of Diabetes", that was recently published in the Canadian Journal of Diabetes Vol 27 Suppl 2 Dec 2003 and is also available to members of the Association on their web site at www.diabetes.ca/cpg2003/download.aspx. (accessed June 06, 2007) and 2) the joint Canadian Diabetes Association – Dietitians of Canada 'Nutrition Labelling Education Centre' at http://www.healthyeatingisinstore.ca/ (accessed June 06, 2007).

18-5 Canadian Resources on Cancer

- The following diet-related health claim linking vegetable and fruit consumption and cancer is now allowed on Canadian foods "A healthy diet rich in a variety of vegetables and fruit may help reduce the risk of some types of cancer".

- Canadian Cancer Society web site - www.cancer.ca/ccs/internet/frontdoor/0,,3172___langId-en,00.html (accessed June 06, 2007)

- Cancer Care Ontario. Insight on Cancer: News and information on nutrition and cancer prevention e.g., Practice Guidelines and Evidence Based summaries by disease at www.cancercare.on.ca (accessed June 06, 2007).

18-6 Complementary / Alternative Therapies and Herbal Medicine in Canada

Since the practice of health professions in Canada is regulated by the provinces, the regulation of groups that practice alternative therapies, such as naturopaths, varies from province to province. There is a growing trend to consider alternative practitioners, such as homeopaths, under health profession regulation to make them more accountable to the public. You can check the regulations for alternative therapists in your province or territory through their respective Ministry of Health web sites.

The Natural Health Products Directorate regulates the quality of natural health products, such as those found in Tables **H18.2** and **H18.3** in the **HIGHLIGHT** for **Chapter 18** in your textbook, and the claims that can be made for them. For current information about the regulations, check their web site: http://www.hc-sc.gc.ca/dhp-mps/prodnatur/legislation/acts-lois/prodnatur/index_e.html (accessed June 06, 2007)

18.7 Canadian Guidelines for Health Promotion

Canada's Guidelines for Healthy Eating were designed to address chronic disease, in general, so they could be a single message for the population[4]. These guidelines are printed in **Table 2.2** in **Chapter 2** of the textbook. For the U.S., the guidelines are presented in **Table 2.1** of the textbook. Canada's guidelines are currently under review, some have already been replaced as the IOM DRI reports. Check the following Health Canada web site for the latest information on these guidelines. http://www.hc-sc.gc.ca/hpfb-dgpsa/onpp-bppn/food_guide_e.html (accessed June 06, 2007).

18-8 Alcohol consumption among students in 40 Canadian Universities (2004)[†]

- 77 % consumed alcohol the month prior to the study
- Males reported drinking more and higher amounts than females
- 18.5 % consumed 5 or more drinks on a single occasion once every 2 weeks or more frequently
- 6.6 % consumed 8 or more drinks on a single occasion once every 2 weeks or more frequently
- almost one third of students reported at least one indicator of dependent drinking (e.g., being unable to stop)

_____

[†] SOURCE: Adapted from the 2004 Canadian Campus Survey
(http://www.camh.net/Research/Areas_of_research/Population_Life_Course_Studies/canadian_campus0905.pdf)

18-9 Eat at Least Two Food Guide Servings of Fish Each Week

- Meat and Alternatives - Eat at Least Two Food Guide Servings of Fish Each Week .
  http://www.hc-sc.gc.ca/fn-an/food-guide-aliment/choose-choix/meat-viande/index_e.html

18-10 Canada Re-Launches ParticipACTION[‡]

According to a February 2007 news release "Canada's New Government recognizes the challenges facing Canada with regard to rising obesity levels and declining physical activity rates, and we know the ParticipACTION name continues to resonate with many Canadians as a motivator to be active" and has earmarked $5 million over the next two years to support the renewal of the program.

[‡] Canada's New Government Re-Launches ParticipACTION

http://www.canadianheritage.gc.ca/newsroom/index_e.cfm?fuseaction=displayDocument&DocIDCd=CHG060916 Feb 19, 2007. Canadian Heritage, Government of Canada.

_____

References Cited

[1]. Statistics Canada: Major Causes of Death – Diseases of the circulatory system
http://www43.statcan.ca/02/02b/02b_003_e.htm   (accessed June 25, 2007)

[2]. McPherson R, Frohlich J, Fodor G, Genest J. Canadian Cardiovascular Society position statement - Recommendations for the diagnosis and treatment of dyslipidemia and prevention of cardiovascular disease _Canadian Journal of Cardiology_ 2006; 22 (11): 913-927.

[3]. Canadian Hypertension Education Program (CHEP). 2007. Recommendations for the management of hypertension: Part 1 – blood pressure measurement, diagnosis and assessment risk. Can J Cardiol Vol 23 (7) 529- 538.

[4]. Health and Welfare Canada. _Action Towards Healthy Eating...Canada's Guidelines for Healthy Eating and Strategies for Implementation._ The Report of the Communications/ Implementation Committee. Ottawa: Minister of Supply and Services Canada, 1990.

Chapter 19 Canadian Information (Consumer Concerns About Foods and Water)

19-1 Agencies that Monitor the Canadian Food Supply

The agencies that regulate the safety of the Canadian food supply at the federal level are shown in Table 19.1 below. These agencies monitor all aspects of food safety, including the use of pesticides, which are primarily regulated by Agriculture and Agri-Food Canada. Provincial departments of health, agriculture and the environment and municipal health departments also share responsibilities for the safety of the food and water supply.

Table 19.1 AGENCIES THAT MONITOR THE CANADIAN FOOD SUPPLY

- **Health Canada**, Health Products and Food Branch – http://www.hc-sc.gc.ca/hpfb-dgpsa/index_e.html
- **Canadian Food Inspection Agency** - http://www.inspection.gc.ca/english/toce.shtml
- **Agriculture and Agri-Food Canada** – http://www.agr.gc.ca/
- **Environment Bureau of Agriculture and Agri-Food Canada** - http://www.agr.gc.ca/policy/environment/home_e.phtml
- **Environment Canada** – http://www.ec.gc.ca/

19-2 Foodborne Illness Outbreak Response Protocol (FIORP):

Canada has had a Foodborne Illness Outbreak Response Protocol (FIORP) in place since the summer of 2004 (updated in July 2006, http://www.hc-sc.gc.ca/ed-ud/respond/food-aliment/index_e.html), a protocol undoubtibly affected by the events of 9/11 and SARS. The Federal, Provincial and Territorial Committee on Food Safety and Policy view it as a 'key procedural document in national emergecy preparedness'

Estimated Number of cases of Foodborne Illness

- Public Health experts estimate that there are between 11 and 13 million cases per year http://www.inspection.gc.ca/english/fssa/concen/causee.shtml

The Canadian Food Inspection Agency also provides information for consumers about the common bacteria, viruses and parasites that cause food borne illness. To find food safety tips and Fact Sheets on how to prevent food borne illness in the kitchen visit the CFIA's website at http://www.inspection.gc.ca/english/fssa/concen/tipcone.shtml .

- For an overview of Canada's BSE safeguards see (http://www.hc-sc.gc.ca/fn-an/securit/animal/bse-esb/safe-prot_e.html).
- CFIA: Kitchen Safety Tips – *Preventing foodborne illness,* available at http://www.inspection.gc.ca/english/fssa/concen/tipcon/kitchene.shtml

In the Fall of 2007, two confirmed cases of botulism in Toronto were associated with the consumption of carrot juice imported from California (see CFIA Health Hazard Alert http://www.inspection.gc.ca/english/corpaffr/recarapp/2006/20061007e.shtml).

- Canadian Food Inspection Agency's Food Safety Facts on Botulism http://www.inspection.gc.ca/english/fssa/concen/cause/botulisme.shtml .

Under the mandatory Food Safety Enhancement Program (FSEP, Nov 2005) all federally registered meat and poultry establishments and storages are being encouraged to implement and maintain this program. (http://www.inspection.gc.ca/english/fssa/polstrat/haccp/manue/app8e.shtml)

19-3 Food Irradiation

Food irradiation is not used as widely in Canada as it is in the United States. Canadian regulations allow for the irradiation of the food items listed in Table 19.2 below. A fact sheet on food irradiation from the Canadian Food Inspection Agency is available at http://www.inspection.gc.ca/english/fssa/concen/tipcon/irrade.shtml (accessed June 26, 2007).

Table 19.2   **Foods approved for Irradiation in Canada‡**

- Onions
- Potatoes
- Whole wheat flour
- Whole and ground spices
- Dehydrated seasonings

‡ SOURCE: modified from CFIA-Food Irradiation http://www.inspection.gc.ca/english/fssa/concen/tipcon/irrade.shtml Nov, 2002.

In addition, Health Canada has **proposed** adding the following to the list of irradiated food permitted to be sold in Canada: fresh and frozen ground beef, fresh and frozen poultry, prepackaged fresh, frozen, prepared and dried shrimp and prawns, and mangoes. Check the following Health Canada website for the status of this proposal http://www.hc-sc.gc.ca/fn-an/securit/irridation/109401_e.html (accessed June 27, 2007).

19-4 Food Additives

Food additives are regulated in Canada under the Food and Drugs Act and Regulations[1]. The approach and regulations are similar to those of the United States. The policy on the use of food additives in Canada is consistent with the FAO/WHO Joint Expert Committee on Food Additives.

The safety of food additives is a concern for individuals with allergies or hypersensitivities. The requirement that all ingredients and food additives be included on labels of prepackaged foods helps these individuals to select foods that they can tolerate. Health Canada publishes warnings with product recalls; foods or beverages are recalled when nuts or other common allergens, are found in them, but are not listed as ingredients. Food recalls, health hazard alerts, safety alerts and allergy alerts can be accessed from the Canadian Food Inspection Agency's website at http://www.inspection.gc.ca/english/corpaffr/recarapp/recaltoce.shtml (accessed June 07, 2007).

19-5 Standards for Organic Foods

The Canadian General Standards Board worked with the Canadian Organic Advisory Board to develop National standards for organic agriculture. For "Frequently Asked Questions" about where the Canadian General Standards Board sits regarding the proposed standards go to the website at http://www.pwgsc.gc.ca/cgsb/on_the_net/032_0310/faq-e.html . For links to the latest proposed documents on Standards regarding Canadian Organic Production Systems e.g., the January 2005 Draft version of the National Standards of Canada, visit the Organic Agriculture Centre of Canada at http://www.organicagcentre.ca/std_canadian.html (accessed June 27, 2007). For a list of links to various organic certification and inspection organizations in Canada visit http://www.gov.mb.ca/agriculture/crops/organiclinks.html . Also, finally, Canada, like the U.S. and various European countries has a "Canada Organic" seal / symbol, that was published in the Canada Gazette in Jan 2007 http://canadagazette.gc.ca/partII/2007/20070124/html/sor10-e.html , although no certification bodies had been approved by the CFIA to use this symbol (see **Figure 19-1**) at the time this book went to publication. In addition, see **Table 19-3** below for the gereral principles of organic production.

Figure 19-1: Canada Organic Logo‡

‡ SOURCE: http://canadagazette.gc.ca/partII/2006/20061221-x6/pdf/g2-140x6.pdf with permission from
the Canada Organic Office, Agri-Food Division, Canadian Food Inspection Agency, Government of
Canada.

Table 19-3 General Principles of Organic Production†

1. protect the environment
2. Maintain long-term soil fertility
3. Maintain biological diversity
4. recycle and maintain resources to greatest extent possible\
5. Provide attentive care to livestock

† SOURCE: modified from Organic Production Systems-Organic Principles and management Standards
ISC 67.040. Canadian General Standard Board, Oct 2005.

19-6 Water Quality in Canada

Water quality is an important issue in Canada, where a number of deaths have been caused by unsafe water supplies. Health and environmental departments of the federal, provincial and territorial governments have responsibilities related to safe water. Health Canada has a web site that reports on water quality activities (http://www.hc-sc.gc.ca/ewh-semt/water-eau/index_e.html).

19-7 Bottled Water in Canada

You can find information about the bottled water in Canada by referring to a fact sheet from the Canadian Food Inspection Agency, "Food Safety Facts on Bottled Water," available at http://www.inspection.gc.ca/english/fssa/concen/specif/bottwate.shtml.

Note: New regulations for Bottled Water are in the final stage of consultation (see http://www.hc-sc.gc.ca/fn-an/consultation/init/bottle_water-eau_embouteillee_tc-tm_e.html) and are expected to be published in Canada Gazette I or II by the end of 2007.

_____

References Cited

[1]. Health Canada's Food Program. *Consolidation of the Food and Drugs Act and the Food and Drug Regulations.* The current regulations can be found at http://www.hc-sc.gc.ca/fn-an/legislation/acts-lois/fda-lad/index_e.html (Accessed July 07, 2006)

HIGHLIGHT 19: Food Biotechnology

H19-1 Genetically Modified Foods in Canada

Health Canada and the Canadian Food Inspection Agency (CFIA) have responsibilities for regulating products derived through biotechnology. Health Canada is responsible for assessing the human health and safety of products derived from biotechnology including foods, drugs, cosmetics, medical devices, and pest control products. CFIA is responsible for regulating products derived through biotechnology including plants, animal feeds and animal feed ingredients, fertilizers, and veterinary biologics. For genetically modified crop plants, CFIA assesses the potential risk of adverse environmental effects and authorizes and oversees import permits, confined trials, unconfined release and variety registration.

The Canadian General Standards Board approved standards for Voluntary Labelling and Advertising of Foods That Are and Are Not Products of Genetic Engineering. These standards were published in April 2004 and can accessed via the Canadian General Standards Board website at http://www.pwgsc.gc.ca/cgsb/on_the_net/032_0315/standard-e.html.

Note: It is mandatory to label all foods that have significant nutritional or compositional changes due to this technology or where health or safety risk exist, such as the presence of an allergen.

You can find current information about genetically modified foods on Health Canada's Novel Foods web site: http://www.hc-sc.gc.ca/fn-an/gmf-agm/fs-if/faq_1_e.html. Thus far in Canada, about 50 genetically modified foods (including corn, canola, soybeans, potatoes, flax, sugarbeets and tomatoes) have been approved by Health Canada for sale in the Canadian marketplace.

Chapter 20 Canadian Information (Hunger and the Global Environment)

20-1 Hunger in Canada

Hunger is a concern in Canada. Poverty among women with young children is one important factor related to hunger. According to the Canadian Council on Social Development (CCSD), in 1999 almost one in five Canadian children lives below the poverty line. http://www.ccsd.ca/pubs/2002/pcc02/hl.htm#es (accessed June 07, 2007). The percentage is even greater for children in single parent households.

Helping at a local food bank, shelter, or emergency feeding centre can provide you with an opportunity to gain an understanding of local hunger issues associated with **food insecurity**.

20-2 Food Security Issues

At the 1996 World Food Summit in Rome, 187 countries including Canada agreed with the following definition for food security: 'Food security exists when all people, at all times, have physical and economic access to sufficient, safe and nutritious food to meet their dietary needs and food preferences for an active and healthy life.'[1] In response to the summit, Canada developed an action plan to deal with food security entitled "Canada's Action Plan for Food Security – a response to the World Food Summit". It is a roadmap to reduce the number of undernourished people by one-half no later than 2015. Canada submitted its second progress report to the Food and Agriculture Organization (FAO) of the United Nations in May 2002 (for the full report see Agriculture and Agri-Food Canada's Food Security Bureau at http://www.agr.gc.ca/misb/fsec-seca/pdf/report-rapport_2_e.pdf). In it, Canada outlined its progress on four of the seven commitments of the Rome Declaration on Food Security as requested by the FAO Committee on World Food Security. Also, at the World Food Summit, participants agreed that a mid-term review be conducted in 2006.

More recently, in March 2005, DC released a position statement entitled "Individual and Household Food Insecurity in Canada: Position of Dietitians of Canada". The full report is available at http://www.dietitians.ca/news/highlights_positions.asp?fn=view&id=3941&idstring=5019%7C3941%7C3398%7C1231%7C2482%7C2175%7C2515%7C1952%7C2516%7C2517%7C1363%7C2451%7C1188%7C1338 although a summary has also been published[2]. According to the report the households most at risk include one-parent families with one or more young children, those receiving social assistance and Aboriginal people living off reserves.

20-3 Canadian Programs Promoting Food Security

According to the Canadian Association of Food Bank's national survey of emergency food programs, HungerCount, the number of food bank users in Canada more than doubled from 378,000 in March 1989 to ~ 825,000 in March 2005. These numbers are released on World Food Day (October 16) each year (753,458 for March 2006); watch for them in the coming year[3]. In addition, the Canadian Living Foundation's 'Breakfast for Learning' program is "Canada's only national, non-profit organization dedicated to supporting child nutrition (http://www.breakfastforlearning.ca/english/index.html). Also, through a network of community breakfast clubs the Children's Emergency Foundation provides help to children living in poverty (http://www.childrensemergencyfoundation.org/). Help from industry is also available, for example, the 'ShareGoods' partnership between the Food and Consumer Products of Canada (FCPC) and the Canadian Association of Food Banks. Last year alone the FCPC "donated over 5 million bags of groceries to families in need" (http://www.fcpc.ca/about/sc/sharegoods.html).

Other Programs include the following:

- Basic Shelf Experience
- Community Kitchens (see Affeldt et al and Marquis et al, below)
- Community Gardens
- FoodShare - http://www.foodshare.net/
- Hunger Project Canada - http://thehungerproject.ca/
- Hunger Relief advisory Committee of London
- Meals-on-Wheels - http://www.mealcall.org/canada/
- School Feeding Programs (see Section 14-4 of this CSI Doc)
- Wheels-to-Meals

Take-home Message: Based on the evaluation of these and other programs, people living on limited incomes are being helped to achieve food security.

20-4 Canadian Readings and Resources

Affeldt T, Thomas H, Vinenti W. Collective Kitchens Handbook. London Community Resource Centre, London ON 2003.

Dewolfe JA, Greaves G. The Basic Shelf Experience: a comprehensive evaluation. *Canadian Journal of Dietetic Practice and Research* 2003; 64(2): 51-57.

Fano TJ, Tyminski SM, Flynn MAT. Evaluation of Collective Kitchens Program: Using the Population Health Model. *Canadian Journal of Dietetic Practice and Research* 2004; 65:72-80.

Marquis S, Thomson C, Murray A. Assisting people with low income: to start and maintain their own community kitchens. *Canadian Journal of Dietetic Practice and Research* 2001; 62(3): 130-132.

Tarasuk V. Household Food Insecurity in Canada. Topics in Clinical Nutrition 2005; 20 (4): 299-312.

References Cited

[1]. Canada's Action Plan for Food Security – a response to the world summit. 1998.
http://www.agr.gc.ca/misb/fsec-seca/pdf/report-rapport_2_e.pdf Agriculture and Agri-Food Canada,
Ottawa (accessed June 07, 2007)

[2]. Individual and Household Food Insecurity in Canada: Position of Dietitians of Canada. *Canadian
Journal of Dietetic Practice and Research* 2005; 66: 43-46.

[3]. HungerCount. 2006. Canadian Association of Food Banks. http://www.cafb-
acba.ca/documents/Hunger_Facts_2006.pdf (accessed June 27, 2007)

HIGHLIGHT 20: Progress Toward Sustainable Food Production

H 20-1 Canada's 4th Sustainable Development Strategy:

According to Agriculture and Agr-Food Canada's 'Sustainable Development Strategy 2007-2009', "In environmental terms, sustainable agriculture and agri-food production is built on the sustainable use of natural resources, such as land, air, water, and genetic resources; the protection of soil, water, and air quality; and the conservation of the rich biodiversity found on agricultural lands and in the wide array of agricultural crops and animals."
(http://www4.agr.gc.ca/resources/prod/doc/policy/environment/pdfs/sds/sds4_e.pdf)

H 20-2 What Can You Do to Help out the Environment ?

 In an effort to help out our environment / reduce our ecological footprint globally (e.g., by eating meat-free meals more often, using less pesticides …), students might consider, from a nutrition standpoint, visiting Dr Suzuki's "David Suzuki Foundation" website and taking the "Nature Challenge" (see http://www.davidsuzuki.org/NatureChallenge/).